SCENES FROM THE PAST 15 : RAILWAYS OI

THE DENBIGH AND MOLD LINE

Denbigh. 19th May 1961. The station building was a striking structure, prominent at the corner of Vale Street, although the beauty of the platform face stonework was somewhat concealed by the canopy that extended the full length of the building and part of the through platform, and also gave some protection to passengers whose train started or terminated in the bay platform. The short spire was reminiscent of school design for the period, and there is some suggestion that it was built for that purpose, but adapted by the Vale of Clwyd Railway, whose headquarters the building was, until that line was absorbed by the London & North Western Railway. The two-arm bracket signal beyond the road overbridge protects the platform road, the lower of the two arms was for the Up and Down Loop line. Facing the photographer are the two starting signals for traffic movements onto the single line and towards Ruthin. *Norman Jones.*

BILL REAR

First Published by Foxline Publishing 1992

ISBN 978 1 907094 82 8

Reprinted June 2012 by Booklaw Publications,
382 Carlton Hill, Nottingham, NG4 1JA

Printed by The Amedeus Press,
Cleckheaton, West Yorkshire, BD19 4TQ

Frontispiece (below). **Nannerch. c.1961**. Branch line stations usually had a rustic charm all of their own, supporting the lie that the job was easy and non-demanding. A solitary wagon of coal for the local merchant stands in the siding. and opposite can just be seen the weigh office. The staff are otherwise occupied and there is an air of timelessness in this beautiful scene, alas no more. The buildings were demolished in a road improvement scheme, and the only surviving relic of this setting is the row of trees. *I. Vaughan.*

The Denbigh and Mold line.

Historical

In May 1845 the Trent Valley Continuation & Holyhead Junction promoters announced the proposal for a railway from Stafford via Wrexham, Mold and Bodfari, to form a junction with the Chester & Holyhead Railway near Abergele. The scheme was subsequently abandoned, but is believed to be the first proposal to construct a line through the town of Mold, and had it come to fruition it would have cut the distance between London and Holyhead by 21 miles.

In the event, it was the Mold Railway Company that constructed a line, of double track, from Saltney Ferry to Mold, a distance of ten miles, under an Act of July 9th 1847. The same Act provided for a branch line to Upper Kings Ferry (subsequently renamed Queens Ferry), which was never built, and to a point near the Ffrith Lime Works near Hope. The Chester & Holyhead Railway was to subscribe £30,000 and the cost of the connection between the two lines was borne by the Mold Railway Company. The authorised capital was £180,000. A tender for its construction was made by Edward Ladd Betts of Peto, Brassey & Betts fame, in November 1846. The following February saw the submission of a tender for £146,130 covering the construction of the main line and the Ffrith branch. This tender was accepted on March 21st when Betts was authorised to make a start on works west of Bramley Lane between the $7^3/_4$ and 8 mileposts - from Chester - as soon as the contract was signed.

By July 1848 work had slowed down, and consequentially, the Chester & Holyhead Company began to show signs of impatience. As a result, work on the Ffrith branch was abandoned beyond the junction at Coed Talon, although this portion was eventually built 33 years later.

It was reported to shareholders on July 10th 1849 that the main line was ready for opening as soon as signals had been provided. A Government Inspector visited the line on August 9th, and gave his blessing. There are conflicting dates in official documents as to the formal opening for traffic, both 14th August and 14th September being quoted, although from the outset, it was worked by the Chester & Holyhead Railway. Before the end of the same year, the undertaking had been absorbed by the C.& H., and was in turn acquired by the London & North Western Railway in 1858.

1. Denbigh. 26th September 1923. A general view of Denbigh station, taken from Fron Fields, looking towards the goods shed. On the left is the siding used by the Timber Yard, which gives some idea of this traffic handled. A high proportion of traffic flowing out from Denbigh came from this yard. In the centre, behind the six wheel coaches can be seen the goods warehouse. In the foreground is the coal siding, with the coal merchants' horses and drays, which were used to deliver coal in the town. On the extreme right is a row of cattle trucks, and which were a regular part of Denbigh goods train traffic. *D.S. Foulkes Roberts.*

The Route Described

The line parted company with the Chester & Holyhead main line on the Down side at Saltney Ferry, (Mold Junction No.1. box), three and a quarter miles from Chester General station. Passenger traffic was served by an island platform opposite the Mold Junction engine shed and passenger access was by steps from the Saltney Lane bridge that crossed the main line. The line then turned south west, with the sorting sidings on the right hand side of the Mold line and motive power depot, yard and access on the left, or Down side. After a short distance the line ascended a gradient of 1 in 270 to reach Broughton & Bretton station, four and three quarter miles from Chester. A private siding to the Premier Artificial Stone Company was located just before the station on the Down side with another serving Vickers Aircraft, subsequently the De Havilland Aircraft Company's Works on the Up side. At Broughton the line crossed the main A55 road (now A5104) on the level and continued climbing to Kinnerton, six and a quarter miles from Chester. The station buildings here were of the standard LNWR 'small station' pattern, of timber construction; the facilities for passengers being somewhat basic. A small goods and coal yard was located on the Up side, with a capacity for fourteen wagons. The line continued climbing, the gradient stiffening to 1 in 43 and 1 in 50, before swinging in a westerly direction to Hope & Penyffordd station (9 miles). Banking of freight trains up the gradient was normal, and Mold Junction shed had several locomotives and sets of men allocated to this work. At Hope & Penyffordd, the line crossed the Hawarden to Wrexham (A550) road on the level beyond the platforms. The bankers came off their trains at this point and after crossing over to the Up line, ran back light to Mold Junction. There were sidings on the Down side for sixteen wagons with provision for six on the Up side. It was intended to make a connection with the Wrexham, Mold & Connah's Quay Railway at this point in 1880, providing through running between Wrexham Central and Chester General stations; some progress had been made with earthworks, when Benjamin Piercy of the W.M.& C.Q.R. died, and the scheme was abandoned.

Now following the course of the River Alyn, the line continued climbing at 1 in 124 to its first summit, at 324ft above sea level near Hope Exchange Low Level Station, nine and a half miles from Chester. At this point the line passed under the W.M.& C.Q.R., now on a falling gradient of 1 in 108. The station had no road connection and existed merely to provide passengers with a convenient transfer point between the respective lines. The platforms were connected by a footpath and a spur line off the W.M.& C.Q. line formed a connection with the Mold Railway on the Down side at Hope Junction. Continuing west, the line maintains the falling gradient for nearly a mile. Just before Padeswood & Buckley station on the Up side, the site of the Padeswood Colliery branch was encountered. A short distance further on was Ffrith Junction where a double track freight only branch left the Down line to connect with the Mold to Brymbo branch line near Coed

2. Denbigh. 26th September 1923. Another view looking towards Denbigh station, this time taken from the Craig Quarry siding line. In the foreground are extensive cattle pens, with a row of wagons behind, most spattered with limewash, which was basically used as a disinfectant. One of Denbigh shed's tank engines shunts the warehouse siding. In the platform, another tank engine stands at the head of a passenger train. On the extreme left hand edge is the back of the No.1 signal cabin. Behind the station the town of Denbigh nestles in the shade of the castle, the roofs of houses on Vale Street in the centre foreground. *D.S. Foulkes Roberts.*

Talon. This branch had closed to traffic before the last war, following the derailment of a freight train. Padeswood closed on 6th January 1958 and was partially demolished within weeks of closure. Three quarters of a mile on was Llong station, situated down a country lane. Before the station was reached however, the line crossed the River Alyn on a cast iron bridge and then the minor road over a hand operated level crossing. The station buildings here, at Broughton & Bretton, and Hope & Penyffordd were designed by Francis Thompson and similar to some small stations on the Chester & Holyhead main line. All three buildings survive to this day. The line now crossed the river twice before Tryddyn Junction was reached, the Mold to Tryddyn branch coming in on the Down side in a trailing direction. Half a mile further on was Mold station, thirteen and a quarter miles from Chester, and was, for twenty years, the terminus of the line. There were extensive facilities here, with siding provision for 127 wagons on the Down side and 104 on the Up.

The Ffrith Branch

The Ffrith branch left the Mold Railway main line 71 chains west of Hope Junction on the Down side and then proceeded south through Coppa Wood to Pontblyddyn, before curving right for Leeswood and Coed Talon East Junction. The branch was short, only two and a half miles in length on a rising gradient of 1 in 33. Double track between Ffrith Junction and Coppa, it became a single line, working on the train staff and ticket system. The branch opened on 14th September 1849 and served the Coppa Colliery. It was closed following an accident on 29th July 1934 when LMS Standard 0-6-0T No.**7374**, working the 4.05pm goods from Coed Talon to Mold Junction and comprising 17 wagons of mineral and two of earthenware drain-pipes, together with the brake van, suffered derailment to the third wagon as the train approached the bridge over the Mold to Wrexham road at Pontblyddyn. In an endeavour to straighten-out the train, the driver applied steam and passed over the bridge safely, but having done so, discovered he had only two wagons attached to the loco. All the others including the brake van had left the rails and gone down the bank, fortunately without injuries. It transpired that the track had spread. The pile-up was cleared over subsequent weeks by the breakdown train, but it was the last working to use the branch, and lifting took place in the spring of 1935. Traffic over the branch had been steady in the early years, with three trains of empties worked to Coed Talon, balanced by three trains of minerals returning to Mold Junction daily. From the terminus at Coed Talon, a private line, known as the Nerquis Private Railway, extended to the collieries of the Nerquis Coal and Canal Company. After the First World War, the frequency gradually diminshed until latterly there was only one daily working each way.

Mold to Brymbo.

The Mold to Tryddyn branch was single track, leaving the main line in a trailing direction at Tryddyn Junction and proceeding due south on a rising gradient for approximately two miles, first on an embankment and subsequently in a cutting. After one and a half miles the gradient eased from 1 in 70 to 1 in 200 for half a mile, during which it crossed the river Terrig on a one arch brick built bridge. The gradient then stiffened to 1 in 70 and changed direction to run east. At this point it was utilising the formation of the Nerquis Private Railway, and continued to Coed Talon West Junction where it joined the Ffrith branch. The summit of the branch was reached at the third milepost and then descended in a south easterly direction at 1 in 130 to Coed Talon station (four and three quarter miles from Mold). Alongside the West Junction to East Junction line was Leeswood Sidings, which held 141 wagons. Immediately beyond the station was a hand operated level crossing and Stuart Colin's Siding, which left off the line which continued to Brymbo. It formed an end-on junction, known as the L.N.W.R. & G.W.R. Wrexham & Minera Extension Joint Railway at 1 mile 15 chains from Coed Talon. When passenger services between Mold and Brymbo ceased in 1951, the line was lifted beyond Stuart Colin's Siding for a distance of two and three quarter miles as far as Bwlchgwyn Siding. Llanfynydd station was six and a half miles from Mold, and Ffrith station a mile further on, where the old lime works were located and the intended terminus of the Ffrith branch. The joint line continued, crossing Nant Ffrith on a stone viaduct to reach Bwlchgwyn Siding. The line then climbed at 1 in 50 for a mile and three quarters in a south easterly direction, crossing another viaduct near Ffrith Hall before finally making a junction with the G.W.R. Coedpoeth and Wrexham line 9 chains north of Brymbo station, located 600ft above sea level on a hillside. The branch from Mold (Tryddyn Junction) to Coed Talon was opened by the LNWR on July 8th 1870 for mineral traffic only, extending to Ffrith and Brymbo on January 27th 1882. Passenger trains did not start running immediately, but commenced between Mold and Coed

3. Bodfari. 23rd August 1961. An afternoon working from Chester to Denbigh comprising a BR Standard 75xxx Class 4 4-6-0 and three non corridor coaches coasts around the curve under the Mold to Denbigh road bridge, and into Bodfari station. *D.S. Foulkes Roberts.*

Talon on 1st January 1892, extending to Brymbo on November 15th 1897. Despite part of it being a joint line, it was worked throughout by the LNWR and its successors. The passenger service was never extensive, in 1922 there being four trains in each direction daily with an extra train each direction on Saturdays. By 1947, this had been reduced to two trips daily in each direction for school children travelling to and from Mold. Traffic rarely justified more than one coach, and was worked by Mold Junction men and engine. Passenger services ceased over the whole of the branch as from 27th March 1950. As with the Mold Railway, the line was worked from the start by the LNWR.

Mold to Denbigh Junction.
Historical.

The Mold and Denbigh Junction Railway was incorporated by Act of 6th August 1861, which authorised the building of a double line fourteen and three quarter miles long from the Mold Railway to Denbigh, on the Vale of Clwyd Railway. Subsequent Acts authorised deviations, abandonments, new lines and additional capital. The company was supported by the LNWR and showed its good faith by paying the parliamentary deposit of nearly £10,000 and sending its own officers to give evidence as to the need for the line before the Select Committee of the House of Commons. During the passage of the bill through Parliament, the LNWR lost interest in the MDJR because of an agreement reached with the Vale of Clwyd Railway and which it absorbed in 1867. The enthusiastic support given to the MDJR initially dissipated and quickly turned to opposition, for apparently, the LNWR had undertaken to arrange construction of the line, but despite frequent reminders, nothing was done, and it appeared that the larger concern was content to let the powers lapse, putting the deposit paid at risk. The MDJR approached Mr Richard Samuel France of Monkland Hall, Shrewsbury, a railway contractor, for help. He attended a fourth meeting of the Board and agreed to construct the line completely, an offer which was taken up by the independent concern. He commenced work almost immediately but discovered that despite the physical connections made, which provided north and south junctions with the Vale of Clwyd, there was no provision for running powers into Denbigh or Trefnant, and the LNWR were not prepared to discuss the impasse. A new Act was obtained on July 5th 1865 which provided for new north and south junctions close to or at Trefnant and Denbigh stations respectively, so as to do away with any need for running powers. Despite this, the lines were not built, and after a tentative approach to the Denbigh, Ruthin & Corwen Railway to create new north and south junctions south of Denbigh station, with suggestions of an amalgamation between the two concerns, the Mold & Denbigh, then applied to Parliament for the necessary running powers, which were granted by an Act of 25th July 1867. However, various devious manouvres, on the part of the LNWR and the Chairman of the House of Lords Committee, which succeeded in the insertion of a clause which rendered the running powers useless, the MDJR was compelled to

4. Denbigh. 27th September 1923. LNWR 'Precedent' Class 2-4-0 no.**1666** *Ariadne* pulls out of Denbigh station with the 12.05pm to Chester, (10.55am from Corwen) comprising five coach set, Circuit No.808 and seen here level with the loco shed. A 2-4-2T stands on the goods siding shunting neck. *D.S. Foulkes Roberts.*

build heavy earthworks on which to construct its own line, 1 mile 9 chains in length from the authorised south junction to Denbigh station, and were driven to purchase house properties on the approaches to the town. Despite all the wheeler-dealing, the MDJR ultimately entered into an agreement with the LNWR - dated 12th November 1868 - and confirmed by LNWR New Works and Additional Powers Act of July 1869 for the working of the former by the latter. As a consequence of this agreement, the authorised line of the MDJR between south junction and Denbigh was to be abandoned. The LNWR for its part agreed to double the Vale of Clwyd line between the south junction and Denbigh; on and after the opening of the MDJR, the LNWR was to operate and maintain the line, provide all rolling stock, staff and stores and work it.

Construction of the line was under the control of George Bellis, the Engineer, subsequently joined on 10th April 1866 by John Ashdown. A scheme which proposed to extend the line to Llandudno was suggested in December 1865, but quickly abandoned. Despite the enthusiasm and input of Mr France, there was a lack of financial support, and during 1867, when construction was at an advanced stage and nearing completion, work ceased. Tenders for the completion of the work were invited, that of Scott & Edwards of Rhyl being accepted, although this was exclusive of stations. These were constructed by Hughes & Son of Mold, who provided four stations and three level crossings with cottages. Stevens & Son of London provided the signals.

The Mold & Denbigh Junction Railway opened for traffic on 12th September 1869, and despite having been worked from the outset by the LNWR, remained independent until the Railways Act 1921 when it was grouped as a subsidiary company in the London, Midland & Scottish Railway.

The Route Described.

After leaving Mold station, the line passed Alyn Tinplate Works siding, one mile from the station, where a signal box with that name stood on the Up side, and which also controlled access to the Synthite Works private siding. The line was now on a rising gradient and headed generally in a northerly direction, following the course of the valley. First station was at Rhydymwyn, sixteen and a quarter miles from Chester, a location where an extensive collection of Government Buildings was built on the Down side in 1940, and the source of much government freight traffic during the latter part of the Second World War. It is believed that 'heavy water' was produced here, and the complex remained rail connected until the freight services to Mold were finally withdrawn and the tracks lifted. It is understood that the sensitive nature of the work done at Rhydymwyn ensured that the site was classified as, and retained as one of strategic importance well into the 1970's. The main station buildings were on the Down side, with the normal freight facilities located on the Up side. The line crossed the main Mold to Denbigh road on the level, a lever frame on the Down platform controlling all traffic movements although the gates were hand operated. On leaving the station the valley closes in and becomes quite narrow. Three quarters of a mile from Rhydymwyn was Dolfechlas Crossing signal box, which protected a minor road leading to the Olwyn Goch lead mine, and the Ruby Brick and Lime Works both of which shared the siding capacity for their own traffic and which was located on the Up side. The box was a standard LNWR design. Eleven hundred yards further on was Hendre Siding signal box, this time on the Down side, and controlling access to the private siding belonging to Hendre Quarries. The valley closed in even more between the two boxes, and the line following the contour, necessitating crossing the

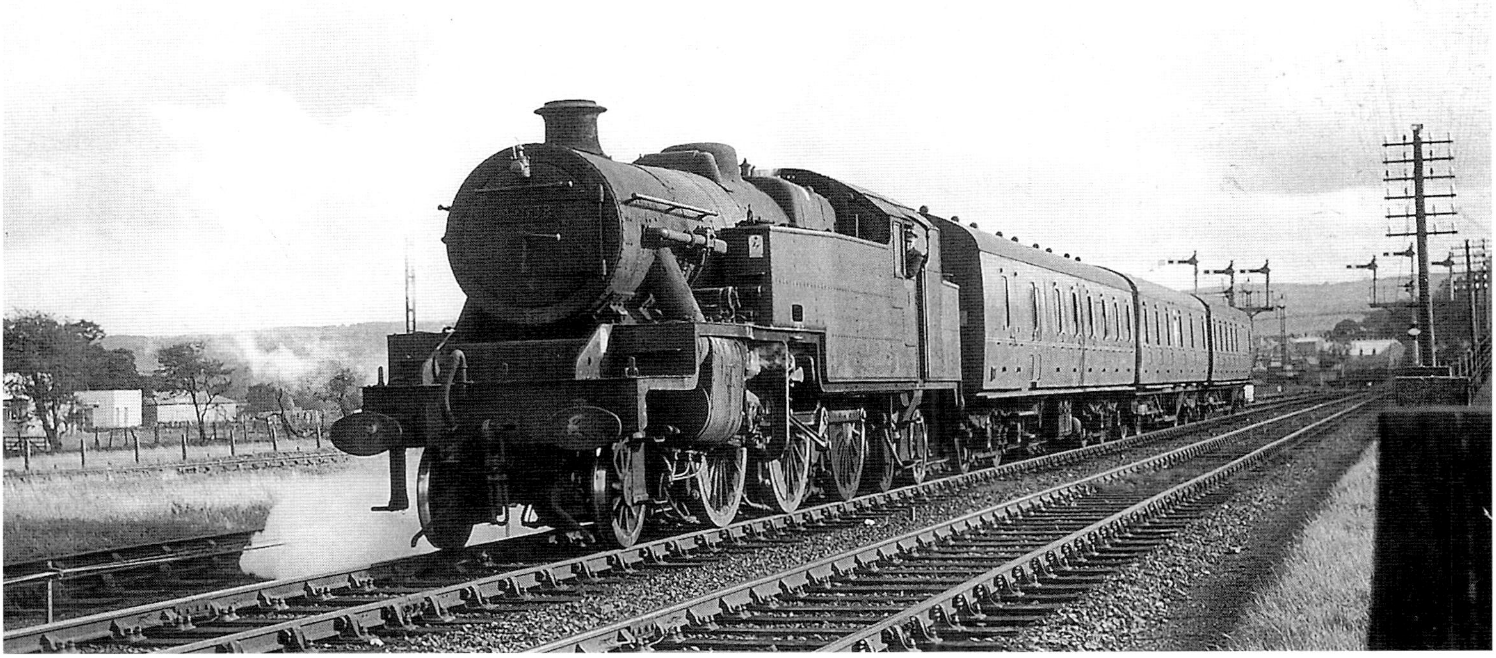

5. Denbigh. 15th August 1961. The 2-6-4T engines working the Chester-Denbigh-Ruthin services were relatively uncommon until the final years of the service, when they replaced the older Class 2P 4-4-0's that had dominated the passenger workings in the immediate post-war period. Here, Stanier Class 4 No.**42538** of Chester shed pulls out of Denbigh with the 12.25pm Ruthin to Chester. The train comprises three non corridor vehicles, the centre coach containing a lavatory compartment. Behind the last coach can be seen the two three-arm gantries that protected the respective Chester & Mold and Rhyl to Denbigh lines, which were parallel single lines from the station to the parting of the ways at the site of Mold & Denbigh Junction signal box, hence the illusion of the train travelling 'wrong line'. *D.S. Foulkes Roberts.*

Mold to Denbigh road twice in rapid succession before the valley widened out once more. Two and a half miles from Rhydymwyn was Star Crossing which comprised simple concrete fronted platforms on both sides. The Up side boasted a small wooden shelter, whilst the Down side had no protection whatsoever. A crossing keeper's cottage stood at the Denbigh end of the Down platform ramp and hand operated gates normally kept across the tracks completed the layout. A room in the cottage served as a booking office and waiting room, passengers crossing to the Down platform over the level crossing. There were no other houses nearby, the nearest village being Cilcain, some two miles distant. Despite the sparseness of habitation, the station remained open until the line closed in 1962.

The summit of the line was reached on the Mold side of Star Crossing Halt. Another mile further on, falling mainly at 1 in 80, Nannerch station was reached, and like Star Crossing, some distance from Nannerch village. The Down platform had a simple shelter whilst the main buildings, which included the Station Master's house, was on the Up side. A small yard with a siding and store shed sufficed at the Mold end for what limited freight traffic emanated from Nannerch. The sidings could hold 17 wagons. The station building was demolished some time after closure to make way for a road widening scheme.

The line kept to the Wheeler valley floor for most of the way, the gradient varying from 1 in 73 to 114 for the next eight miles and heading north west before reaching Caerwys station, 23 miles from Chester. The main buildings were on the up side, and true to form the village of Caerwys was about a mile from the railway, although there were houses around the station and the settlement is known as Afonwen. There was substantial freight traffic despatched from here, mainly timber, and a large goods shed stood on the Down side at the Mold end of the platform. Bodfari, 25½ miles from Chester had the main buildings on the Up side, the line running into the station under the road bridge carrying the Mold to Denbigh road. The goods yard was at the Denbigh end of the platform, also on the Up side and could hold 21 wagons. Immediately on leaving the station inthe Denbigh direction, the line commenced climbing for the next 1½ miles to 'Blue Hand' bridge, which carried the St.Asaph to Bodfari road over the line and in the early days of operation was a constant source of trouble before eventually being taken down and rebuilt. Just beyond the bridge the line levelled off, before descending towards Denbigh for a mile prior to climbing once more at 1 in 96 to the junction with the Vale of Clwyd line. Until 28th April 1957 the line was double track throughout. From that date, the Down line from Bodfari to the Junction with the Vale of Clwyd line, together with the junction connection and Mold & Denbigh Junction Signal Box, were taken out of use. The disused track was lifted shortly afterwards. The layout from the junction was modified to two single lines running parallel as far as the station throat. The new Denbigh Station signalbox controlled all station movements.

The line had an uneventful life, never achieving its full potential, although there was sufficient freight traffic to and from Mold to justify its retention after the passenger traffic ceased on 30th April 1962. The tracks were lifted between Denbigh and Dolfechlas signal box and the remaining double track was singled from there to Mold and then to Hope Junction, to the spur connecting the line with the Wrexham Central to Bidston line. The track from Hope Junction to Mold Junction was lifted. Regular traffic to Mold survived for a while, but gradually deminished, the last freight train finally ran on 15th March 1983. The track was lifted from Mold back to the Padeswood Cement Works siding in 1985.

6. Denbigh. 21st April 1962. Fairburn Class 4 2-6-4T No.**42229** of Chester shed (6A) comes off the Rhyl line onto the Up & Down Loop line outside Denbigh Station signal box, the Rhyl fireman exchanging tokens with signalman W.O. Hughes. It then ran through the loop to couple with the stock that formed the 4.00pm to Ruthin. For some reason the loco is carrying Class 'J' lamps although on this day the crew worked light engine from Rhyl. In the background can be seen an ex LMS brake van, standing on what was once the turntable road. Above the roof of the hut and the van can be seen the Graig Quarry line, which climbed and turned through almost ninety degrees. This locomotive had transferred from Corkerhill, Scottish Region, to Chester on 6th February 1960, and remained there until withdrawn in the week commencing 18th January 1964. In this penultimate Saturday before closure the engine diagrams had been distorted by Easter traffic. The rostered duty was nominally Mold Junction diagram Turn 10, for a BR Standard Class 4 4-6-0, but this had been requisitioned at Rhyl for a job to Chester, replacing another Class 4 75xxx which had failed, the 2-6-4T being substituted at the last minute. Rhyl men, 6K Turn No.27, worked the turn to Ruthin and back to Denbigh, before being relieved by Rhyl Turn 33 at 4.45pm who took the train on to Chester. The first crew returned to Rhyl by bus. *Norman Jones.*

Train Services.

The earliest working time table available is dated **August 1862**, and passenger workings and coal traffic between Chester and Mold are shown separately. There were four passenger trains daily in each direction, leaving Mold at 8.00am, 11.00am, 4.30pm and 7.15pm, taking forty minutes for the journey. All trains called at Llong, Padeswood, Hope, Broughton Hall and Chester. Departures from Chester were at 9.30am, 2.30pm, 5.40pm and 8.15pm. A goods train left Chester at 10.40am daily, arriving at Mold at 11.31am. It returned from Mold at 1.15pm and arrived back in Chester at 2.20pm. It called at all passenger stations and also at Mold Junction and Betts Hall on the return working. On Sundays there were two passenger trains in each direction, departing Mold at 8.50am and 6.15pm, and Chester at 9.45am and 7.20pm. The passenger services were worked from Mold where a locomotive depot was provided. A M&DJR Minuted reference dated 20th June 1869 proposed locating an engine turntable at Mold to be provided by the LNWR, but this came to nothing.

Seven coal trains in each direction are shown working between Chester and Padeswood, with another two coal trains each way to and from Broncoed Colliery at Mold. Four of the trains starting from or finishing at Mold Junction, where there was extensive siding facilities. There were no Sunday freight trains over the branch.

The locomotive depot at Mold Junction had not yet been built, and engines worked to and from Chester shed to take up, and on finishing their rostered work. The early working time tables do not show light engine movements.

When the Mold & Denbigh Junction railway was opened, the time table structure was recast; Mold shed was closed and the work transferred to Denbigh and Chester. The locomotive shed was converted into a warehouse. Works Committee Minute No.16346, dated 17th June 1874 refers, amongst other things, to the floor of the Engine Shed being made suitable for warehousing grain, and a window opening being made into a door.

Mold Junction locomotive depot opened on 1st October 1890, principally handling the freight traffic of the District and the North Wales coast, with the Mold and Denbigh line coal traffic working transferred there from Chester. There was also some limited local passenger work based at Mold Junction, principally covering the service between Mold and Brymbo through Coed Talon.

There is no evidence to suggest that passenger trains ever worked over the Padeswood to Coed Talon branch.

The next working time table to hand dates from **July 1904**, and by which time all the branch lines are operational. Passenger trains took seventy three minutes on average for the 29 mile journey between Chester and Denbigh. There were seven passenger trains daily in each direction (but only six SO), the fastest train being the 6.18pm from Chester which ran non stop to Mold and after a two minute wait continued express to Denbigh, arriving there at 7.10pm. There was one working SX and two SO between Mold and Denbigh, and one passenger SX, two SO between Mold and Chester. Most of the Down freight workings were shown as 'conditional' with four running from Mold Junction to Denbigh, the remaining workings terminating at Mold. The Up freight workings were similar. There were no Sunday trains.

Two goods trains each way were shown working over the Padeswood, Coppa & Coed Talon branch for the same period, although the timings of the Up trains varied between weekdays and Saturdays. On the Mold, Coed Talon & Brymbo branch, there were four passenger trains each way, daily, and an extra train each way on Wednesday and Saturday evenings. A freight train ran from Mold to Coed Talon daily, where it re-grouped before working forward as a 'Joint Goods', to Brymbo, disposing of its stock and collecting a fresh load before working back to Coed Talon. It shunted there for seventy five minutes before returning to Mold. Again, there were no Sunday trains.

By **July 1919** the passenger service over the line remained largely unchanged with seven trains each way between Chester and Denbigh and return. A 'motor train' now ran twice daily between Denbigh and Mold, and the listed freight workings were fewer, although to be fair, the 'conditional' prefix had been removed from most of them. One ordinary goods and one 'fast goods' worked through from Mold Junction to Denbigh, the former taking five hours twenty five minutes for the journey, stopping most stations, and waiting forty minutes at Padeswood and another hour at Mold. There were two freight workings to Coed Talon daily. The early morning empties trip worked first to Mold where it reversed, the second train working via Padeswood and Coppa. In the reverse direction a goods train left Denbigh at 1.00pm and shunted all sidings and stations to Nannerch, then called at the Ruby Brick Works on advance notice being given before 11.00am, then Rhydymwyn and Mold, where it waited fifty minutes before working to Padeswood and then non stop to Mold Junction. On the Brymbo branch, there were five passenger trains daily each way between Mold and Brymbo and return. An

7. Near Bodfari. 8th September 1961. The track between Bodfari and Caerwys was straight for most of the way, only changes in the rising gradient providing some variety. Here, a Chester train climbs steadily, approaching Bodfari Down distant signal. In the distance, the chimney for the former foundry at Caerwys is just visible. *D.S. Foulkes Roberts.*

interesting feature was the daily working of a GW light engine which departed Brymbo 3.50am arriving Mold 4.17am. to work the early morning train for workmen to Brymbo at 4.32am., and repeated the working in reverse in the afternoon, departing Brymbo with the workmens' train at 3.15pm SX (3.10pm SO), arriving Mold at 3.45pm (3.36pm SO). The locomotive then worked back LE at 4.08pm to Brymbo, due there at 4.33pm. There were no through freight or mineral workings, Coed Talon being the terminal point. However, it would seem that the locomotive that worked the 11.10am passenger from Mold, parked its coaching stock at Brymbo and worked the 11.50am mineral to Coed Talon, returning from there with the 1.15pm mineral to Brymbo, in time to work the 2.20pm passenger back to Mold. Probably some of the timing delays were to facilitate train crew changes.

On the Padeswood, Coppa and Coed Talon branch, traffic had dwindled to one train each way, daily, departing Mold Junction at 11.40am, and reaching Coed Talon at 1.30pm, after a wait of 45 minutes at Coppa. It then worked a short trip back to Coppa at 2.40pm, returning to Coed Talon after fifteen minutes for traffic purposes. It then departed Coed Talon at 3.30pm for Mold Junction, pausing for ten minutes at Coppa to uplift any wagons, and another ten minutes at Padeswood, before working through to Mold Junction without any booked stop en route.

There were cosmetic changes to the Working Time Table in the **July 1st 1923** issue under LMS Control, in that the timing pages now showed services from Chester and Rhyl through to Corwen, the Padeswood, Coppa and Coed Talon; and the Mold to Brymbo workings on the same pages whereas formerly these were shown separately. This may have been necessary prior to 1923 in that the Mold & Denbigh Junction Railway still existed as a separate concern, albeit worked by the LNWR, but was included in the amalgamation legislation to regularise the situation.

8. Rhydymwyn. 28th August 1961. A BR Standard Class 4 4-6-0 heads a three coach train of non-corridor stock from Chester to Ruthin, and is seen here approaching the Down Distant signal. During the last war, the Ministry of Defence established a factory alongside the line on the Down side, considerable traffic being carried to and from this unit.
D.S. Foulkes Roberts.

The first summer season under LMS control showed a substantial increase in the service, with eleven trains each way between Chester and Denbigh, one between Chester and Mold and three between Denbigh and Mold with some of the workings extended to and from Ruthin or Corwen. A 'motor' or two coach push and pull train worked extensively from Denbigh, and worked The 8.07am to Mold, returning at 9.00am, then worked the 9.55am to Chester from Denbigh and the 11.55am return.It then worked the 2.07pm and 5.15pm to Mold, returning from there at 4.07pm and 6.15pm

On the Brymbo branch, there were four through passenger trips SX and an extra late evening working on Saturdays each way and one short unbalanced working departing Coed Talon at 8.25am for Mold, worked by the Denbigh motor train set, probably for school children. The GWR locomotive workings for the workmen's trains from Mold to Brymbo and return had gone, but GW engine and men now worked an early morning mineral empties from Brymbo to Coed Talon and returned with a mineral train to Brymbo (MX). The freight trips between Mold and Coed Talon had been further reduced to two each way daily, whilst the Coppa branch working remained unchanged.

The period of the General Strike saw the service drastically curtailed to five trains each way between Chester and Denbigh. The Brymbo branch was reduced to three trains daily between Mold and Brymbo, and four trains in the reverse direction.

The service frequency was unchanged by September 1926 although there were minor timing changes.

By **May 1934** the passenger service frequency had increased to thirteen trains daily (SX) between Chester and Denbigh with an additional late night train on Saturdays, and the Brymbo branch had gained an extra train daily, making five return journeys on weekdays and six on Saturdays. Freight services remained virtually unaltered, apart from minor timing changes. The Coppa branch closed following the accident mentioned previously.

As Britain gradually came out of the depression, the service increased again, reaching its peak frequency in the high summer period for 1939 with the same number of weekday trains between Chester and Denbigh, but on Saturdays this increased to fifteen trains each way. Sunday trains ran too, with five through trains each way. On the Brymbo branch, the weekday frequency remained at five trains each way, increasing to eight on Saturdays. There were no Sunday trains. Freight traffic had increased slightly and the same period showed three through freight workings between Mold Junction and Denbigh, and two in the reverse direction, with some additional trips worked part way. Passenger working timetables for the summer 1939 period have been reproduced on pages 18-20.

The outbreak of World War II saw a drastic reduction in passenger services, and the emergency timetables introduced on 11th September 1939 saw the service cut back to six trains between Chester and Denbigh and return each week day, with an additional train on Saturdays. There was one train each day between Chester and Mold and return, and the Brymbo branch was reduced to three trains each way daily. This was eased slightly, the working time table commencing **October 28th 1940** listing seven trains each way weekdays, and ten on Saturdays. The Chester to

Mold and return working had gone, and the Brymbo branch was reduced to two trains each way. By **1943** the weekday frequency had increased to eight trains each way, with no change on the Brymbo branch. There was a reduction of one train each way by **October 1945** between Chester and Denbigh.

The first summer after nationalisation saw eleven passenger trains between Chester and Denbigh each weekday, but only nine in the reverse direction. The Brymbo branch service survived with two trains each way, Mondays to Fridays, mainly for school children travelling to and from Mold. Two freight trains ran daily each way between Mold Junction and Denbigh, with two additional workings between Mold Junction and Mold and return. There was one freight working along the Brymbo branch, worked with the same engine that operated the passenger service - generally one of Mold Junction's Class 4F 0-6-0 tender engines - was to be found on the job. Some interchange mineral traffic came off and for the Wrexham, Mold & Connah's Quay line at Hope Junction, starting from and terminating at Mold Junction sidings, and there was some traffic between the Cement Works at Padeswood but generally traffic was declining even at this early stage.

Regular passenger traffic between Mold and Brymbo ceased in March 1950 whilst services between Ruthin and Corwen ceased on 23rd January 1953 following which some Chester to Denbigh trains were now extended to Ruthin. The **Summer 1954** working time table showed ten trains from Chester to Denbigh or Ruthin, and one between Mold and Denbigh during the week, and one working from Mold to Rhyl via Denbigh on Saturdays. In the reverse direction there were nine between Denbigh and Chester, with one working from Denbigh to Mold SX and an ECS working on Saturdays Only, to take up the Mold to Rhyl working. Two freight trains ran daily each way between Mold Junction and Denbigh. There were three freight workings between Mold Junction and Mold, one of which worked a trip to Coed Talon and back, whilst a second working ran from Mold to Hendre Quarry and back.

This pattern remained broadly the same for both passenger and freight traffic until the closure of branch lines gathered momentum. The summer service for **1960** saw nine trains daily between Chester and Denbigh or Ruthin, with an extra working between Mold and Denbigh and return although the timings of this short working were different on Saturdays. In the opposite direction there was one train less. From **1961** the line was under threat, so much so that the Section D Passenger Working Time Table omitted to include it in that edition, but because an objection to closure was lodged, BR was obliged to issue a supplement listing the timings, which were broadly the same as the previous summer, and were similarly unbalanced. The same thing happened when the winter schedules were announced, and again the passenger services were omitted from the timetables although the Freight Time tables were included. There were no through freight services between Mold Junction and Denbigh, but there was an Up working departing Denbigh at 6.36pm that worked through to Mold Junction SX. A Class H freight worked to Mold arriving there at 7.13am, and after shunting, worked to Coed Talon and back. After another fifteen minute wait, it returned to Mold Junction with a Class J freight. A Class K working left Mold Junction at 9.23am and worked to Mold, where it shunted for two and a half hours before continuing to Hendre Siding. After a brief wait it returned to Mold before shunting for seventy nine minutes prior to moving back to Mold Junction. A Class K freight left Denbigh at 10.38am (SX) and worked to Nannerch where it waited thirty minutes before returning at a leisurely pace to Denbigh. The passenger services finally ceased on Saturday 28th April 1962 although freight continued to be worked to and from Mold. The **September 1963** Freight Book shows two trains daily. The first one arrived Mold at 7.13am and after shunting made a trip up the Coed Talon branch and back SX. It returned to Mold Junction at

9. Hope & Penyffordd. 10th July 1948. From about 1946, the LMS Class 2P 4-4-0 locomotives were used on most passenger services between Chester, Denbigh and Corwen, and were ideally suited to haul the two coach non-corridor sets that made up most of the workings. Here, No.**M671** of Rhyl shed (7D), stands at the Up platform on the 2.25pm Corwen to Chester working. The locomotive was normally based at Denbigh, and upon closure of that shed remained for a few weeks at Rhyl before transferring to Chester. *W.A. Camwell.*

10.25am. The second train left Mold Junction at 9.30am and shunted at Mold from 10.19am until 12.40pm when it worked to Rhydymwyn. It worked as required there, probably including a trip to Hendre Sidings as required, and departed from Rhydymwyn at 2.36pm. (One hour earlier SO). More shunting at Mold followed, before it departed at 3.45pm for Mold Junction. The Summer of 1964 saw the Coed Talon trip omitted, the loco shunting at Mold for nearly three hours before returning. The second engine worked as before, although running 90 minutes later than the previous year, and proceeding to Rhydymwyn after forty five minutes shunting. Departure from there was as before. By **1965** these freight workings were omitted from the Working Time Tables, but were included in the District Shunting and Trip Working Books, although the Freight WTT books still showed the line in the schematic map and continued to do so until 1970. Although the tables were included, no timings were given, but indicated that such timings were included in the local trip working books. Gradually this work diminished and succumbed to the inevitable, traffic finally ceasing in 1983.

Non-Passenger Traffic.

The railways were common carriers until the imposition was relaxed and removing the burden that this imposed, was one of the better pieces of railway legislation. Until this obligation was repealed, provision was made by all companies for the transport of every type of commodity. Certain classes of traffic was conveyed in non passenger carrying stock, of which the Royal Mail was probably the best known, and which the travelling public saw as a matter of course on train journeys. All companies and subsequent regions had some dedicated non-passenger carrying trains for this specific purpose. The rural branch line had no need for complete trains, and usually a van attached to specific working sufficed to carry the traffic to the distribution centres and terminal points. Mailbags carried on the rural branch lines were under the eye of the passenger guard, and loading and unloading was generally undertaken by Post Office staff.

The 'News', or Newspaper traffic was an intensive user of the railways, with complete trains operating from the main centres of population to the suburbs and furthest reaches of the country. Again, the branch lines catered for the reduced amount handled. The LMS issued specific instructions for the conveyance of parcels traffic to and from stations in booklet form, entitled *Instructions for Dealing with Parcels Traffic*, and produced booklets for each of the four operating divisions, the Western Division book dated November 1938 and coded as ERO 21229, which advised all staff that the arrangements 'must be strictly observed'. The first two pages outlined the procedures, such as 'labelling of vans, Chalking vans, searching vans, sectionalising traffic, traffic over-carried, damaged parcels, affixing of parcels stamps etc., as well as routing for parcels traffic and restrictions to ordinary parcels. The bulk of the booklet listed the specific workings of Up and Down line parcels trains, the majority apparently converging on Euston, although some were routed to other destinations, like Birmingham, Crewe, etc. A summary list was provided at the beginning, and details of the make-up of each train listed, specifying the type of vehicle, its destination and time of arrival. The point where vans were detached and routed via other services was given. Each table then indicated the position of consignments within each van. It would seem that traffic to and from Mold did not warrant a through van, and parcels traffic was transferred at Chester to the care of the guards on local passenger trains. Traffic for Denbigh and the Vale of Clwyd was routed via Rhyl and similarly transferred to ordinary passenger workings.

Distinct from the parcels and mail traffic, provision was made for small consignments to be conveyed along branch lines by Tariff vans, which were attached to regular workings and in most cases ran daily. Details were given in the publication *List of Tariff Vans*, ERO 29536, and extracts in this instance are taken from an edition dated July 1935. In the Down direction, van numbers **146**, labelled to Corwen, and serving Llanrhaiadr, Rhewl, Ruthin, Eyarth, Nantclwyd, Derwen, Gwyddelwern and Corwen, and van **148**, labelled to Denbigh and serving Mold Junction, Rhydymwyn, Nannerch, Caerwys, Bodfari and Denbigh departed at 9.25pm from Chester to Mold Junction. They were attached to the 5.50am from Mold Junction to Denbigh. Van **146** worked forward with the 9.43am to Corwen. Van **149** was also labelled to Denbigh, and also departed Chester on the 9.25pm to Mold Junction, but it was then worked to Rhyl on the 1.40am (MX) from Mold Junction (3.05am MO), and the 6.00am from Rhyl to Denbigh. Van **300** from Liverpool Park Lane was labelled to Corwen and was attached to the 1.05am from Edge Hill to Mold Junction, and thence on the 5.50am from there to Denbigh, in company with vans 146, 148; and kept company with van 146 to Corwen. Van **301** also departed from Edge Hill at 1.05am to Mold Junction, and was labelled Denbigh via Mold. However it did not work forward to Mold until 10.43am, and served Broughton & Bretton, Kinnerton and Hope. It then worked forward to Denbigh on the 2.53pm from Mold, and served Rhydymwyn, Nannerch, Caerwys and Bodfari. Van **315** ran from London Broad Street on the 9.47pm to Camden and then on the 10.30pm Camden to Mold Junction in the company of van **326** from Camden, both labelled to Corwen, and worked forward from Mold Junction on the 9.15am to Mold, the 2.53pm to Denbigh and the 9.10am to Corwen (next day). These vans served every station between Mold Junction and Corwen with the exception of Hope Exchange, Llong and Star Crossing. Van **347** departed from Manchester Liverpool Road at 9.20pm for Mold Junction and was labelled to Bodfari. It was included with the 10.40am from Mold Junction to Mold, and then went forward on the 2.53pm, and served the same stations as 315 and 326 together with traffic for Coed Talon and Llanfynydd, on the Brymbo branch, which was transferred at Mold into van no.**154**. Van **154** had departed Chester at 9.25pm and Mold Junction for Mold at 8.05am, labelled to Llanfynydd, and had gone forward from there at 1.10pm. Van **155,** meanwhile labelled Mold, had departed Chester on the 9.55am to Rhyl as far as Mold Junction, then transferred to the 10.40am to Mold and called at the principal stations. Van **350**, also from Manchester Liverpool Road, where it departed at 9.20pm for Mold Junction, was labelled to Corwen, and was attached to the 5.50am from there to Denbigh, and thence on the 9.43am to Corwen, calling at all stations.

In the Up direction, and presumably using the same vans, No.**189** departed from Denbigh at 12.20pm for Mold Junction and was labelled to Chester, serving most stations to Mold then Chester. Van **438** labelled to Chester departed Ruthin at 9.25am for

Denbigh, and worked forward at 3.30pm to Chester, calling at most stations, attached to a passenger train working.
The railway involvement continued with its own distribution system, conveying traffic, large or small, from the nearest railhead to its final destination. The road motor fleet was an integral part of this service, and usually these penetrated the furthest points away from the station or goods yard. The LMS had its 'Country Lorry' Service, with lorries based at Chester, Mold and Denbigh, and which operated the collection and delivery service to and from most stations along the line. The Commercial Manager for the Chester District supervised the needs of each station on a daily basis, and scheduled the lorry duties accordingly. The maroon LMS Country Lorry was a familiar site at all the stations along the line. The service was continued after Nationalisation, although some of the specialist traffic was hived off to British Road Services. The railway continued to operate its own lorry service dealing with parcels traffic for several years, until the staffing levels of stations was reduced and eventually disappeared.

Freight Traffic.

All but the smallest stations were provided with facilities for handling freight traffic. In the early days, there was considerable coal traffic from the Mold area, but as the pits became worked out, or uneconomic to work, the traffic fell away, and had all but disappeared at the time of the 1923 Grouping. Once this had ceased, the surviving freight traffic was of a mixed variety, mainly livestock and agricultural produce, with timber, mineral and domestic coal constituting the major commodities carried. By way of example, the **July 1904** working time table showed paths for 17 mineral or empties trains, fourteen of them 'Conditional' between Mold Junction and Hope Junction and most destined for the Great Central (formerly the Wrexham, Mold & Connah's Quay Railway) line, although only one is shown working forward to Coed Talon. Two more trains worked to Mold, neither conditional, whilst another four trains worked through to Denbigh, of which one was conditional. In the reverse direction, four trains worked from Denbigh through to Mold Junction, of which one was conditional, two more trains worked back from Mold and seventeen worked from Hope Junction to Mold Junction, (two from Coed Talon) of which fifteen were conditional.
By **July 1919**, freight traffic had dwindled to a shadow of its former self, mainly due to the removal of conditional trains from the working timetable and drastic reduction of interchange traffic at Hope Junction to three trains daily during the week and an extra early morning train on Saturdays. There was one working each way along the Coppa branch to Coed Talon, two to Mold, which extended back to Coed Talon, one slip trip between Mold and Hendre Siding, and two through trains between Mold Junction and Denbigh. The Down workings balanced the Up trips, although there were some timing differences on Wednesdays between Mold and Mold Junction with the return Coed Talon-Mold-Mold Junction working.
The summer **1939** working time table showed little change from that of twenty years earlier, apart from traffic to and from Coed Talon which was now worked through Mold. The Hendre Sidings trip was now extended to Caerwys, and ran on Mondays, Wednesdays and Fridays only. Two trains worked between Mold Junction and Denbigh each way each day, and there were five trains each way between Mold Junction and Hope Junction for interchange with the LNER line.
There was little variation after the war, and the Summer **1949** freight timetable showed two through trains each way between Mold Junction and Denbigh, although the trip from Mold to Caerwys had been cut back to Hendre Siding but now ran daily.
By **June 1954** the services had modified somewhat. The Brymbo branch had been truncated just beyond Coed Talon. The first train of the day, a Class 'H' working, reporting number 40, departed Mold Junction at 5.15am, halted briefly to detach at Hope Junction and Mold and then worked through to Denbigh, taking 40 minutes from Mold. This was a Mold Junction working, diagrammed for a 4F 0-6-0, but almost anything could be pressed into service, and crew and loco went on shed to turn, returning home with the 8.35am Class 'K' working, departing Denbigh at 8.35am and calling briefly at to uplift stock from Bodfari, Caerwys, Rhydymwyn, Mold, Hope Junction and Broughton & Bretton before reaching Mold Junction at 11.49am.
A second Class 'H' departed Mold Junction, reporting number 41, at 5.55am running as far as Mold. After shunting there from 6.57am until 10.00am it worked to Coed Talon, departing from there back to Mold at 11.10am. The engine then ran light back to Mold Junction at 1.00pm.
A second Class 'H' through working from Mold Junction to Denbigh, reporting number 62, and another Class 4F diagram, departed there at 9.23am calling at Hope Junction, Mold, Nannerch, Caerwys and Bodfari, reaching there at 12.04pm. The loco went on shed after parking its stock, the men working home on a passenger turn. A second Mold Junction set worked out passenger from Chester to Denbigh, and after taking over the same engine, departed Denbigh at 6.43pm working under Class 'H' lamps, reporting number 58. This worked non-stop to Mold, with only a seven minute stop to take on water. Apart from stopping to pin down brakes at the head of Kinnerton bank, it only called briefly to uplift traffic at Broughton & Bretton before pulling into Mold Junction yard at 8.32pm.
A Class 'K' freight worked out of Mold Junction yard for Hendre Siding at 10.40am and shunted every yard in between, which it reached at 12.56pm. It then departed tender first back to Mold at 1.42pm and called at North Hendre Siding and Rhydymwyn. It shunted at Mold until 5.30pm when it resumed the journey back to Mold Junction. There was some exchange traffic at Hope Junction, and on average, three trains daily worked between Mold Junction and there. The practice was to assist trains up Kinnerton bank as far as Hope Junction, and after detaching there, work traffic off the former LNER line back to Mold Junction yard.
By **June 1957**, traffic had dwindled to four trains between Mold Junction and Mold. Two of them worked through to Denbigh and return, in much the same timings as 1954. The second freight train of the day ran to Mold, where it shunted, and worked the Coed Talon trip. The fourth working was to Hendre Siding, returning as before. The same arrangement for working exchange traffic off the LNER line persisted.
Timing details of Shunting Engine work at Mold and Denbigh were given in the Chester District Operating Superintendent's booklet, (ERO 53002/6) '*Shunting Engine and Local Trip Notice*, issued coincidentally with the working time tables.

Coach Working.

The coaching stock used on the Chester to Denbigh line, in common with most of the North Wales Coast branches, was non corridor local stock, and confined to Chester District. As far as can be seen, there was no through working of coaches outside the district, and no mention of any through coach working can be found in the Passenger Train marshalling books available. Details of the local circuit stock used over the line was printed in *Diagram of Carriage Working* books, issued three times a year and timed to coincide with the schedule changes in the Working Time Table and Passenger Train Marshalling books (for Main Line workings), issued in April, July and September each year, up until 1933, when printing of these local coach working books discontinued, replaced by Roneo Duplicated Sheets. Nevertheless these continued to follow the same pattern of issue and did so until the outbreak of World War II in September 1939 when their issue varied according to the traffic requirements and restrictions imposed by the war. Afterwards Working Time Table and Passenger Train Marshalling publications were issued twice a year until 1965, by which time all passenger traffic on the line had ceased. The earliest *Diagram of Carriage Working* to hand dates from **21st September 1925**. The Mold to Coed Talon and Brymbo service was worked by sets 796-8, shown as 3 vehicles - 39 tons, and was based on Chester for servicing, whilst the chained-up sets that worked between Chester and Denbigh were listed as Llandudno District sets numbered 807-817, comprising 5 vehicles 65 tons, and working a six day cycle. Set 851 was a motor train set consisting of a Driving Third, and strengthened by circuit set 852 (corridor third) on certain days. In addition, some strengthening sets were included on various services, and these varied from one to three six wheel coaches on circuits 835, 836 and 843. Full details of these circuit workings are given below.

COED TALON SETS

(3 vehicles - 39 tons)

No.796 - Worked by No.798 (M) and No.798(MO)

	arr a.m.	dep a.m.	
Chester	..	7.38	A.
Mold	8.24	...	

A - 2K and R van extra.
Works No.797 (M) and No.797(MO)

No.797 - Worked by No.796 (M) and No.796 (MO)

	arr a.m.	dep a.m.	
Mold	..	8.00	
Brymbo	8.26	10.00	
Mold	10.26	11.10	
Brymbo	11.36	2.30pm	
Mold	2.56pm	3.30	**SO**
Brymbo	3.56	5.32	**SO**
Mold	5.58	4.20	**S**
Brymbo	4.48	5.00	**S**
Mold	5.26	7.28	
Brymbo	7.54	8.15	
Mold	8.41	9.05	**SO**
Brymbo	9.33	10.20	**SO**
Mold	10.46		

Works No.798 (M) and No.798 (MO)

No.798 - Worked by No.797 (M) and No.797 (MO)

	arr a.m.	dep a.m.	
Mold	..	8.00	
Coed Talon	8.10	8.26	
Mold	8.36	8.40	A.
Chester	9.29	2.15pm	A.
Denbigh	3.22pm	3.28	A.
Corwen	4.21	5.00	A.
Chester	7.33		

Works No.796 (M) and No.796 (MO)

LLANDUDNO DISTRICT SETS

(5 vehicles - 65 tons)

No.807 - Worked by No.807

	arr a.m.	dep a.m.	
Chester	..	6.35 **S**	A.
Holywell Jn.	7.15	5.25pm **S**	A.
Chester	6.10pm		

A. - N extra
Works No.807.

No.808 - Worked by No.812 (M) and No.812 (MO)

	arr a.m.	dep a.m.	
Chester	..	6.52	A.
Denbigh	8.30	9.10	
Corwen	10.07	10.55	B.
Chester	1.18pm	2.35pm	
Birkenhead	3.29	3.53	
Chester	4.40	8.12	
Denbigh	9.35		

A. - R. extra Corwen
B. - Two N extra, Mold to Chester (SO)
Also road van for Rhyl from Ruthin to Denbigh (S).
Works No.810 (M) and No.810 (MO).

No.809 - Worked by No.813 (M) and No.813 (MO)

	arr a.m.	dep a.m.	
Corwen	..	8.05	
Denbigh	9.01	9.06	
Rhyl	9.33	10.00	A.
Abergele	10.07	**10.15**	A.
Rhyl	**10.22**		

A. (MO) also on third Wednesday in each month
Works No.816 (M) and also first Wednesday in each month excepted
Works No.813 (MO) also first Wednesday in each month

No.810 - Worked by No.808 (M) and No.808 (MO)

	arr a.m.	dep a.m.	
Denbigh	..	6.33	C.
Chester	8.08	1.15pm	
Denbigh	2.35pm	2.40	
Ruthin	3.54	4.30	D.
Denbigh	4.48	4.53	B.
Rhyl	5.22	6.05	
Denbigh	6.35	6.42	
Ruthin	6.56		

B - N extra (WO)
C - Van each Birkenhead and Lime St.
D - N extra (SO) to Rhyl
Works No.817 (S) and No.812 (SO)

No.811 - Worked by No.817 (M) and No.817 (MO)

	arr a.m.	dep a.m.	
Denbigh	..	7.35	A.
Chester	8.43	8.52	
Mold	9.33	10.00	
Chester	10.34	1.00pm **S**	
Birkenhead	1.52pm	2.15 **S**	
West Kirby	3.11	3.20 **S**	
Birkenhead	4.11	4.45 **S**	
Chester	5.25	6.00 **S**	
Ruthin	7.29	8.20 **S**	
Denbigh	8.36	9.12 **ThO**	
Rhyl	9.42	10.30 **ThO**	
Denbigh	11.00		
		noon	
Chester	..	12.00 **SO**	
Rhyl	1.30		

A - LK extra Chester
Works No.814 (M) and No.815 (MO)

No.812 - Worked by No.816 (S) and No.810 (SO)

	arr a.m.	dep a.m.	
Denbigh	..	7.40 **S**	
Ruthin	7.54	8.05	
Denbigh	8.23	8.35	A.
Chester	9.39	10.20	B.
Corwen	12.57pm	1.32pm	
Denbigh	2.19	2.55	
Rhyl	3.25	4.23	
Denbigh	4.55	5.15	
Corwen	6.12	7.00	
Denbigh	7.50	8.10	
Chester	9.30		

A - Also road van Chester (S)
B - LK extra Denbigh
Works No.808 (M) and No.808 (MO)

No 813 - Worked by No.814 (M) also first Wednesday in each month excepted
Worked by No.809 (MO) also first Wednesday in each month

	arr a.m.	dep a.m.	
Rhyl	..	9.00 **MO**	B.
Denbigh	9.33	9.50 **MO**	B.
Ruthin	10.04	**10.10 MO**	B.
Denbigh	**10.22**	1.24pm	
Rhyl	1.56pm	2.40	
Denbigh	3.10	4.57	
Chester	6.08	6.32	A.
Denbigh	7.55	8.00	
Corwen	8.55		

A - Birkenhead to Denbigh
B - Also first Tuesday in each month
Works No.809 (M) and No.809 (MO)

No.814 - Worked by No.811 (M) and No.815 (MO)

	arr p.m.	dep p.m.	
Denbigh	..	3.20	A.
Chester	4.40	5.15	
Denbigh	6.24		

A - Also road van Corwen to Chester (S)
Works No.813 (M) and No.816 (MO)
Also first Wednesday in each month.

No.815 - Worked by No.811 (SO)

	arr a.m.	dep a.m.
Rhyl	..	6.00 **SO**
Chester	7.35	8.28 **SO**
Holywell Jn.	9.10	11.50 **SO**
Chester	12.39pm	1.00pm**SO**
Birkenhead	1.52	4.45 **SO**
Chester	5.25	6.00 **SO**
Ruthin	7.29	8.20 **SO**
Denbigh	8.36	9.12 **SO**
Rhyl	9.42	10.30 **SO**
Denbigh	11.00	

Works No.814 (MO)

No.816 - Worked by No.809 (M) also first Wednesday in each month excepted
No.814 (MO) also first Wednesday in each month

	arr a.m.	dep a.m.	
Rhyl	..	9.00 **M**	A.
Denbigh	9.31	10.00	
Rhyl	10.29	10.55	B.
Denbigh	11.25	11.55	
Rhyl	12.24pm	1.23pm	
Denbigh	1.53	2.24	
Chester	3.13	4.30 **SO**	C.
Hooton	4.52	**5.00 SO**	
Birkenhead	**5.16**	6.06 **SO**	
Helsby	6.54	7.05 **SO**	
Birkenhead	8.01	8.35 **SO**	
Chester	9.03	9.25	C.
Denbigh	10.42		

A - Also first Tuesday in each month
B - N extra (WO)
C - Two N extra (SO)
Works No.812 (S) and No.817 (SO)

No.817 - Worked by No.810 (S) and No.816

	arr a.m.	dep a.m.	
Ruthin		7.15 **S**	A.
Denbigh	7.31	7.47	
Rhyl	8.16	8.31	
Denbigh	9.03	9.10	
Chester	10.15	10.20	
Birkenhead	11.10	11.23 **S**	
West Kirby	12.15pm	12.25pm**S**	
Birkenhead	1.17	3.13	
Chester	3.58	4.25	A.
Denbigh	5.56	6.05	
Rhyl	6.37	7.05	
Denbigh	7.38	8.05	
Rhyl	8.36	9.10	
Denbigh	9.41	9.50 **SO**	
Ruthin	10.04	10.13 **SO**	
Denbigh	10.29		

A - Also R Rhyl
Works No.811 (M) and No.811 (MO).

No.835 - LK

	arr a.m.	dep a.m.
Denbigh	..	7.35 **S**
Chester	8.43	6.00pm **S**
Denbigh	7.25pm	

No.836 - O, K and N.
(six-wheeled vehicles - 39 tons)

	arr a.m.	dep a.m.	
Denbigh	..	8.25	
Ruthin	8.39	10.25 **ThS** (freight)	A.
Denbigh	10.40	...	
Ruthin		9.50 **ThO**	
Denbigh	10.06	...	
Ruthin		9.27	*
Corwen	10.07	10.55	*
Denbigh	11.47	12.00pm	*
Corwen	12.57pm	1.32	*
Denbigh	2.19	2.40	*
Ruthin	2.54	4.30	*
Denbigh	4.48	...	
Ruthin		1.00pm **SO**	
Denbigh	1.19		

A - Also first Tuesday in each month excepted
* - First Tuesday in each month

No.843 - N - 13 tons

	arr a.m.	dep a.m.
Rhyl	..	5.20 **SO**
Denbigh	5.50	6.05 **SO**
Ruthin	6.50	4.30pm**SO**
Rhyl	5.22pm	

MOTOR TRAINS
MOLD AND DENBIGH BRANCH

No.851 - Driving third (27 tons), on extra vehicle (WSO) (27 tons)

	arr a.m.	dep a.m.	
Rhyl	..	5.20	
Denbigh	5.50	6.28	
Rhyl	6.55	7.30	
Denbigh	8.00	8.07	
Mold	8.48	9.02	
Denbigh	9.41	9.55	
Chester	11.18	11.55	
Denbigh	1.15pm	1.58pm	A.
Mold	2.39	4.07	A.
Denbigh	4.45	6.33 **S**	
Rhyl	7.02	...	
Denbigh	..	5.15 **SO**	
Mold	5.56	6.15 **SO**	
Denbigh	6.53	7.10 **SO**	
Rhyl	7.41		

A - C, F extra (WO)

No.852 - CF - 28 tons

	arr a.m.	dep a.m.
Rhyl	..	10.55 **WO**
Denbigh	11.25	1.58pm**WO**
Mold	2.39	4.07 **WO**
Denbigh	4.45	4.53 **WO**
Rhyl	5.22	

In the above tables, F - Bogie Third, K - Composite, L - Bogie First, LK - Composite (Lavatory), M - First Class, N - Third Class, O - Third Brake, R - Brake Van.

It will be noted that one coach set (No.813) stopped overnight at Corwen at this time. The LMS locomotive department had a presence there, which they shared with the GWR, who closed the shed in 1927. After that date the time table was recast, and LMS trains started and finished their day's work at Denbigh.

By 1933, the oldest vehicles had been replaced and the five coach six wheel non corridor stock had given way to two coach non corridor sets. Nevertheless the stock used over the Chester to Denbigh line remained local, working under the Llandudno District heading as before, a state which persisted until the closure of the line. There is reason to believe that the same circuit numbers were in use until the end. As before, there was no regular through working of coaching stock into or out of the district.
The set numbers and workings for the period 17th July to 10th September 1933 period were listed as **Llandudno District Sets**, and were listed as Circuit Set Nos.819 to 832. The workings now included trips to Whitchurch as well as to Birkenhead, although there was no work to Hooton or West Kirby in this block. The **Coed Talon Set.** was shown as 2 vehicles - 26 tons, so presumably must have been six wheel stock, and carried circuit numbers 805-7, the latter taking a trip to West Kirby on a Saturday afternoon. The strengthening sets had increased in number, and were listed as nos.843-850/7, Set 856 was a strengthening set for the Brymbo branch, and Motor Train set No.871 worked between Denbigh and Mold and return.
In common with most rural lines before the Second World War, increasing prosperity, as the recession receded, generated more leisure travel, which the LMS exploited. Apart from the seasonal Sunday School Excursions to the seaside, full and half day cheap-rate tickets were offered on most trains outside the peak hours, and at week-ends, special cheap-day excursion trains were laid on. Two typical examples of additional excursion traffic is shown below, taken from the RDS Carriage Working for Special and Additional Trains booklet (ERO 53022/3) for the period from Friday July 22nd to Thursday July 28th 1938. The first (**445**) was a regular Saturday excursion to Rhyl commencing at Padeswood, with the stock utilised for an extra train to Chester, whilst standing at Rhyl. The second (**452**) was a Sunday School Excursion.

445	Lavatory EE.T. (7 B)				
	circuit 2123	a.m.	a.m.		
	Chester	...	9.55	**E**	**186**
	Padeswood & B. ...	10.22	10.30	**X**	
			p.m.		
	Rhyl	11.43	4.40	**E**	
		p.m.			
	Prestatyn	4.47	4.50	**SO**	
	Chester	5.55	...	**E**	
	Rhyl	...	7.55	**X**	
	Padeswood & B. ...	9.10	9.15	**E**	
	Chester	9.37	...		663a
452	Loose stock (3 B).	a.m.	a.m.		
	Mold	...	9.25	**E**	
	Brymbo	9.48	10.30	**SSX**	
			p.m.		
	Rhyl	11.53	9.05	**SSX**	
		p.m.			
	Brymbo	10.37	11.15	**E**	
	Mold	11.40	...		
	70 adults, 100 ch.				

Post War Coach Working

Some information has come to light about the composition of passenger traffic between Chester and Denbigh, taken from the LMS and GW Joint Railways booklet listing the Arrival and Departure of Passenger Trains at Chester (General) Station, publication ERO 53085, dated October 6th 1947. Details are abstracted from the relevant pages.

Down Trains departing Chester.

5.40amMO	Denbigh	IDZ 3 coach set. Off 6.45pm Whitchurch
MX	Denbigh	2 coach set. Off H.& C. ex Rhyl (SX) Coed Talon set. (SO). Off 7.50am Ruthin (SO)
7.20amMO	Corwen	IDZ 3 coach set. Off 1.25pm Rhyl (Sun)
MX	Corwen	2 coach set. Off 9.45am Denbigh.
7.40am	Broughton	3 coach set.
9.00am	Denbigh	2 coach set. Off 6.45am Ruthin. Due 8.31am
10.25am	Corwen	2 coach set. Off 7.50am Ruthin. Due 9.24am
12.45pmSO	Denbigh	2 coach set. Off 9.45am Denbigh. Due 11.00am
1.10pmSX	Denbigh	2 coach set. Off 10.03am Rhyl. Due 11.10am
2.10pmSO	Denbigh	2 coach set. Off 10.55am Corwen. Due 1.12pm
3.40pmSX	Denbigh	2 coach set. Off 1.07pm Denbigh. Due 2.20pm
4.15pmSO	Denbigh	2 coach set. Off 1.40pm Corwen. Due 3.58pm
5.05pmSX	Broughton	2 coach set. Off 2.25pm Corwen. Due 4.41pm
5.42pm	Denbigh	2 coach set. Off 4.35pm Birkenhead. Due 5.30pm
6.20pmSX	Corwen	2 coach set. Off 5.40pm Broughton. Due 5.52pm
SO	Corwen	2 coach set. Off 4.55pm Denbigh. Due 6.09pm
8.10pmSX	Denbigh	2 coach set. Off 5.50pm Denbigh. Due 7.08pm
SO	Denbigh	2 coach set. Off 1.07pm Denbigh. Due 2.20pm
9.35pm	Denbigh	2 coach set. Off 6.50pm Corwen. Due 9.03pm

Up Trains arriving Chester.

7.15am	Mold	2 coach set. Due 7.53am. Works 8.25am Rhyl.
6.45am	Ruthin	2 coach set. Due 8.31am. Works 9.00am Denbigh
8.30am	Broughton	2 coach set. Due 8.41am. Works 7.40am Broughton next day.
7.50am	Ruthin	2 coach set. Due 9.24am. Works 10.25am Corwen
9.45am	Denbigh	2 coach set. Due 11.00am. Works 7.20am Corwen next day
10.55amSX	Corwen	2 coach set. Due 1.12pm. Works 3.20pm Birkenhead
10.55amSO	Corwen	2 coach set. Due 1.12pm. Works 2.10pm Denbigh SO
1.07pmSX	Denbigh	2 coach set. Due 2.20pm. Works 3.40pm Denbigh SX
1.07pmSO	Denbigh	2 coach set. Due 2.20pm. Works 8.10pm Denbigh SO
1.40pmSO	Corwen	2 coach set. Due 3.58pm. Works 4.15pm Denbigh SO
2.25pmSX	Corwen	2 coach set. Due 4.41pm. Works 5.05pm Broughton
5.40pmSX	Broughton	2 coach set. Due 5.52pm. Works 6.20pm Corwen SX
4.55pmSO	Denbigh	2 coach set. Due 6.09pm. Works 6.20pm Corwen SO
5.50pmSX	Denbigh	2 coach set. Due 7.08pm. Works 8.10pm Denbigh SX
6.50pm	Corwen	2 coach set. Due 9.03pm. Works 9.35pm Denbigh

Accidents.

There have been few accidents of note recorded on the line, although inevitably there have been mishaps attributed to one cause or another. Basic details of those have been abstracted from John Dixon's book *19th century British Railway Accidents,* published by the author in early 1992. On 12th May 1856 a collision occurred at Broughton, probably due to an under-powered engine stalling on Kinnerton bank, with another on the Mold branch on 11th December 1857, when the 9.15am passenger train from Chester ran into the back of a mineral train on Kinnerton bank.

It would seem that there were no further reportable incidents in the 19th century, and comparatively little untoward happened to draw attention to the line until 13th April 1936, when George V Class 4-4-0 No.**5343** *Otterhound* broke the trailing coupled axle whilst starting away from Caerwys. There were no casualties, apart from the locomotive. In the last weeks of operation, a fatal accident occurred when a young lady was struck down by a Chester to Denbigh train at an occupation crossing between Nannerch and Caerwys.

10. Caerwys. 24th April 1936. 'George V' Class 4-4-0 No.**5343** *Otterhound,* whilst working a train from Chester to Denbigh suffered a most unusual mishap, in that the trailing coupled axle broke whilst pulling away from the station. The mishap, which was most unusual and fortunately very rare, blocked the Up and Down lines until the breakdown gang could be taken to the scene. They managed to get the engine into the Up side siding at the Denbigh end of the station. *J.M. Dunn.*

11. Caerwys. 24th April 1936. George V Class 4-4-0 No.**5343** *Ottherhound* in the Up side siding at Caerwys, being hoisted in the air by the breakdown crane whilst a replacement set of wheels were fitted. The job took five hours, and after which, the engine was towed to Denbigh shed. The cause of the mishap was a spring steel frame of the oiling pad had broken, and acted as a cutting tool on the axle, scoring a groove about $^1/_4$inch deep, which flawed the axle. Llandudno Junction breakdown crew were in attendance. *J.M. Dunn.*

CORWEN, DENBIGH, RHYL, MOLD, COED TALON, BRYMBO, AND CHESTER.

WEEKDAYS.

Miles		Station	1	2	3	4	5	6	7	8	9	10	11	12	13	14	15	16	17
			MOTOR TRAIN.	PASSENGER.	PASSENGER.	PASSENGER.	PASSENGER.	MOTOR TRAIN.	PASSENGER.		PASSENGER.	PASSENGER.	PASSENGER.	PASSENGER.	PASSENGER.	PASSENGER.	PASSENGER.	PASSENGER.	PASSENGER.
					SO	ThO	Th SX											SO	SX
			a.m.	a.m.	a.m.	a.m.	a.m.	a.m.	a.m.		a.m.	a.m.	a.m.	a.m.	a.m.	a.m.	a.m.	p.m.	p.m.
		CORWEN ⊕ dep.									8 10					10 55			
		Gwyddelwern ⊕ arr.																	
2½		Gwyddelwern ⊕ dep.									8 16½					11 2			
5¼		Derwen							See note A		8 22					11 7			
		Nantclwyd ⊕ arr.																	
7¼		Nantclwyd ⊕ dep.									8 26					11 13			
10¼		Eyarth									8 32					11 20			
		Ruthin ⊕ arr.									8 36					11 23			
12		Ruthin ⊕ dep.		6 58					8 7		8 39		9 25			11 26			
13½		Rhewl		7 2					8 11		8 43		9 29			11 30			
15½		Llanrhaiadr		7† 8					8†17		8†49		9†35			11†36			
		DENBIGH ⊕ arr.		7 14					8A25		8A57		9 41			11A44			
18¾	0	DENBIGH ⊕ dep.	6 30	7 16	7 30	7 41	7 54	8 14	8 30		8 59	9 6	9 50	9 55	10 35	11 47	11 51	12 28	12 40
19½	1	Denbigh Junction ⊕	6*33	7 19	7*33	7*44	7*57	8 17	8 33		9* 2	9 9	9*53	9 58	10*38	11 50	11*54	12*31	12*43
		Trefnant ⊕ arr.	6 37		7 37	7 48	8 1				9 6		9 57		10 42		11 58	12 35	12 47
	2¾	Trefnant ⊕ dep.	6 38		7 38	7 49	8 3				9 7		9 59		10 43		11 59	12 36	12 48
		St. Asaph ⊕ arr.	6 43		7 43	7 54	8 8				9 12		10 4		10 49		12 5	12 41	12 54
	5	St. Asaph ⊕ dep.	6 46		7 44	7 55	8 9				9 14		10 5		10 50		12 6	12 42	12 55
	7½	Rhuddlan ⊕	6 51		7 49	8 0	8 14				9 19		10 10		10 55		12 11	12 47	1 0
	10	Foryd Junction ⊕	6*55		7*53	8* 4	8*18				9*23		10*14		10*59		12*15	12*52	1* 4
	11	RHYL arr.	6†57		7 55	8 6	8 20				9 25		10 16		11 1		12†17	12 54	1 6
22½		Bodfari dep.		7 24				8 21½	8 37½			9 13½		10 3		11 55			
25		Caerwys	PASSGR.	7 31	PARCELS.		PASSGR.	8 28	8 44			9 20		10†11	PASSGR.	12 2			
28½		Nannerch		7 41				8 36	8 52			9 28		10†22		12 10			
29½		Star Crossing						8 39½						10 26					
31½		Rhydymwyn		7 48				8 44	8 58½			9 35		10 31		12 17			
		MOLD arr.	a.m.	7 53	a.m.		a.m.	8 49	9 3			9 40		10 36	a.m.	12 22			
34½	0	MOLD dep.	7 30	7 56	7 40		8 3		9 9			9 41		10 40	11 8	12 23			
	½	Tryddyn Jn. ⊕			7*42		8* 5								11*10				
	4½	Coed Talon ⊕ dep.			7 51		8 14				See note A				11 19				
	6½	Llanfynydd			7 54		8 17								11 22				
	7½	Ffrith					8 20								11 25				
	8¾	BRYMBO ⊕ arr.			8 0		8 26								11 31				
36½		Llong dep.	7 34	8 0										10 44		12 27			
37½		Padeswood & Buckley	7 36½	8 3								9 47		10 47		12 30			
		Hope Exchange arr.	7 40	8 6										10 50		12 33			
38½		Hope Exchange dep.	7 40½	8 7										10 51		12 34			
39		Hope & Penyffordd	7 42½	8 10					9 19			9†52		10 54		12 37			
41¾		Kinnerton	7 47½	8 16					9 24					11 0		12 43			
43¼		Broughton & Bretton	7 51	8 20					9 27½					11 4		12 47			
		Saltney Ferry	7 54½	8 24					9 31					11 8		12 51			
44¾		Mold Junction No. 1 pass	7X56	8X25					9X32			10X 3		11X 9		12X52			
46		Saltney Junction	7 58	8 27					9 34			10 5		11 11		12 54			
48		CHESTER arr.	8 2	8 31					9 38			10 9		11 15		12 58			
		Notes	†—P.B. 6.59 a.m. (MO). One Class only.	†—Arrives 7.6 a.m.				One Class only.	†—Arrives Llanrhaiadr 8.15.		†—Arrives Llanrhaiadr 8.47 a.m.	†—3 minutes recovery time, Hope & P. to Mold Jn. No. 1.	†—Arrives 9.33 a.m.	†—Arrives Caerwys 10.9, and Nannerch 10.20. One Class only.	To run on Saturdays only after Sept. 9th. One Class only.	†—Arrives Llanrhaiadr 11.34.	†—On Saturdays runs 1 minute later, Foryd Junction to Rhyl. Public Bills 12.21 p.m. (SX).		Not to run after September 9th.

Miles		Station	18	19	20	21	22	23	24	25	26	27	28	29	30	31	32	33	34
			PASSENGER.	PASSENGER.	PASSENGER.	PASSENGER.	PASSENGER.	Light Engine.	PASSENGER.	PASSENGER.	PASSENGER.	PASSENGER.	PASSENGER.	PASSENGER.	PASSENGER.	PASSENGER.	PASSENGER.	PASSENGER.	PASSENGER.
				Th SX	Th SO	Th SO		SO	SX		SO			SX	SO	SO		SX	SO
			p.m.	p.m.	p.m.	p.m.	p.m.	p.m.	p.m.	p.m.	p.m.	p.m.	p.m.	p.m.	p.m.	p.m.	p.m.	p.m.	p.m.
		CORWEN ⊕ dep.							1 37		1 50								
		Gwyddelwern ⊕ arr.																	
2½		Gwyddelwern ⊕ dep.							1 44		1 57								
5¼		Derwen							1 49		2 2								
		Nantclwyd ⊕ arr.																	
7¼		Nantclwyd ⊕ dep.							1 54		2 7								
10¼		Eyarth							2 1		2 14								
		Ruthin ⊕ arr.							2 4		2 17								
12		Ruthin ⊕ dep.	12 20	1 5		1 25			2 5		2 18						4 35		
13½		Rhewl	12 24	1 9		1 29			2 9		2 22						4 39		
15½		Llanrhaiadr	12†30	1†15		1†35			2†15		2†28						4†45		
		DENBIGH ⊕ arr.	12A38	1A23		1 41			2 21		2 34						4 51		
18¾	0	DENBIGH ⊕ dep.	12 45	1 30	1 30	1 45	1 50		2 25	2 40	2 45	3 35	3 45	4 23	4 23		4 55	5 0	5 0
19½	1	Denbigh Junction ⊕	12 48	1*33	1*33	1*48	1 53		2 28	2*43	2 48	3 38	3*48	4*26	4*26		4*58	5 3	5 3
		Trefnant ⊕ arr.		1 37	1 37	1 52				2 47			3 52	4 30	4 30		5 2		
	2¾	Trefnant ⊕ dep.		1 41	1 41	1 54				2 48			3 53	4 32	4 32		5 3		
		St. Asaph ⊕ arr.		1 46	1 46	1 59				2 53			3 58	4 37	4 37		5 8		
	5	St. Asaph ⊕ dep.		1 47	1 47	2 1				2 54			4 0	4 40	4 40		5 9		
	7½	Rhuddlan ⊕		1 52	1 52	2 6				2 59			4 5	4 45	4 45		5 14		
	10	Foryd Junction ⊕		1*58	1*58	2*10				3* 3			4*11	4*49	4*49		5*18		
	11	RHYL arr.		2B 0	2† 0	2B12				3† 5			4 13	4 51	4†51		5A20		
22½		Bodfari dep.	12 53				1 58		2 33		2 53	3 43						5 7½	5 8
25		Caerwys	1 0				2 5		2 40	Light Engine.	3 0	3 50	PASS.	PASSR.				5 14	5 15
28½		Nannerch	1 10				2 15		2 50		3 10	4 0						5 22	5 25
29½		Star Crossing					2 19												
31½		Rhydymwyn	1 17	See note A			2 24		2 57	SX	3 17	4 7	SO	SX				5 28½	5 32
		MOLD arr.	1 22				2 29		3 2	p.m.	3 22	4 12	p.m.	p.m.				5 33½	5 37
34½	0	MOLD dep.	1 24				2 30	2 55	3 4	3 15	3 24	4 16	4 20	4 30		5 25		5 35½	5 39
	½	Tryddyn Jn. ⊕											4*22	4*32					
	4½	Coed Talon ⊕ dep.											4 31	4 41					
	6½	Llanfynydd											4 34	4 44					
	7½	Ffrith											4 37	4 47					
	8¾	BRYMBO ⊕ arr.											4 43	4 53					
36½		Llong dep.	1 28				2 34					4 20						5 39½	5 44
37½		Padeswood & Buckley	1 31				2 37					4 23				5 32		5 42	5 47
		Hope Exchange arr.	1S034									4 26						5 45	5 50
38½		Hope Exchange dep.	1S035									4 27						5 47	5 52
39		Hope & Penyffordd	1 38				2 42					4 30						5 49	5 56
41¾		Kinnerton	1 44				2 48					4 36						5 54½	6 3
43¼		Broughton & Bretton	1 48				2 52					4 40						5 57½	6 8
		Saltney Ferry	1 52				2 57	3 25		3 45		4 44				5 43		6 2	
44¾		Mold Junction No. 1 pass	1X53				2X58		3X17		3X37	4X45				5X44		6X 3	6X14
46		Saltney Junction	1 55				3 1		3 19		3 39	4 47				5 46		6 5	6 16
48		CHESTER arr.	1 59				3 5		3 23		3 43	4 51				5 50		6 9	6 20
		Notes	†—Arrives 12.28 p.m.	†—Arrives Llanrhaiadr 1.13. To run daily commencing September 11th. B—Public Bills 2.1 p.m.	Not to run after September 9th. †—Public Bills 2.1 p.m.	†—Arrives Llanrhaiadr 1.33 p.m. Not to run after September 9th. B—Public Bills 2.16 p.m.	One Class only.		†—Arrives Llanrhaiadr 2.13.	†—2 mins. later, Foryd Jn. to Rhyl, on Sats., July 15th to August 12th inclusive. P.B. 3.7 p.m. Daily.	†—Arrives 2.26 p.m.		Arrives Foryd Jn. 4*9 p.m. One Class only.	Not to run after September 8th. One Class only.	†—Public Bills 4.55 p.m.		†—Arrive Llanrhaiadr 4.43 p.m. A—Public Bills 5.23 p.m. (SO).		

Corwen Branch—Passenger trains cannot cross at Gwyddelwern or Nantclwyd.
Vale of Clwyd Branch—Passenger trains cannot cross at Rhuddlan.
Brymbo Branch—Passenger trains cannot cross at Coed Talon.

A—Two minutes allowed to run through loop at Denbigh.

321

CORWEN, DENBIGH, RHYL, MOLD, COED TALON, BRYMBO, AND CHESTER.

WEEKDAYS—continued.

Station	35	36	37	38	39	40	41	42	43	44	45	46	47	48	49	50	51	52
	PASSENGER.	PASSENGER.	PASSENGER.	PASSENGER.	PASSENGER.	PASSENGER 4.55 p.m. from Brymbo.	MOTOR TRAIN.	PASSENGER.	PASSENGER.	PASSENGER.	PASSENGER.	Light Engine.	PASSENGER.	PASSENGER.	PASSENGER.	PASSENGER.	PASSENGER.	PASSENGER.
	SO	SX	SX	SO	SO	SO		SX	SO			SX			SX		SX	SO
	p.m.	p.m.	p.m.	p.m.	p.m.	p.m.	p.m.	p.m.	p.m.	p.m.	p.m.	p.m.	p.m.	p.m.	p.m.	p.m.	p.m.	p.m.
CORWEN ⊕ dep.			5 0	5 0									6 50					
Gwyddelwern ⊕ arr.																		
Gwyddelwern ⊕ dep.			5 7	5 7									6 57					
Derwen			5 12	5 12									7 2					
Nantclwyd ⊕ arr.																		
Nantclwyd ⊕ dep.			5 18	5 18									7 8					
Eyarth			5 25	5 25									7 15					
Ruthin ⊕ arr.			5 28	5 28									7 18					
Ruthin ⊕ dep.			5 29	5 29						7 8	7 8		7 25				8 35	8 40
Rhewl			5 33	5 33						7 12	7 12		7 29				8 39	8 44
Llanrhaiadr			5†39	5†39						7†18	7†18		7†35				8†45	8†50
DENBIGH ⊕ arr.			5 45	5 45						7 24	7 24		7A43				8 51	8 56
DENBIGH ⊕ dep.	5 30	5 50	5 54	6 0	5 54	6 12	6 45	6 50	6 50	7 35		7 40	7 47	8 0	8 10	8 30		
Denbigh Junction ⊕	5*33	5*53	5 57	6* 3	5 57	6*15	6*48	6 53	6 53	7*38		7*43	7 50	8* 3	8*13	8*33		
Trefnant ⊕ arr.	5 37	5 57		6 7		6 19	6 52			7 42				8 7	8 17	8 37		
Trefnant ⊕ dep.	5 41	5 58		6 8		6 23	6 53			7 43		7*47		8 8	8 18	8 38		
St. Asaph ⊕ arr.	5 46	6 3		6 13		6 28	6 58			7 48				8 13	8 23	8 43		
St. Asaph ⊕ dep.	5 47	6 4		6 15		6 29	6 59			7 49		7*52		8 14	8 24	8 46		
Rhuddlan ⊕	5 52	6 9		6 20		6 34	7 4			7 54		7*57		8 19	8 29	8 51		
Foryd Junction ⊕	5*56	6*13		6*24		6*39	7* 8			7*59		8* 2		8*23	8*33	8*55		
RHYL arr.	5 58	6 15		6 26		6 41	7 10			8 1		8 5		8 25	8 35	8 57		
Bedfari dep.			6 2		6 2			6 58	6 58				7 55					
Caerwys			6 9		6 9			7 5	7 5				8 2			Light Engine		
Nannerch			6 19		6 19			7 15	7 15				8 12					PASSENGER.
Star Crossing								7 18½	7 18½							W		W
Rhydymwyn			6 26		6 26			7 23	7 23				8 19			SX		SO
MOLD arr.			6 31		6 31			7 28	7 28				8 24			p.m.		p.m.
MOLD dep.			6 33		6 33			7 31	7 43				8 26			8 40		9 0
Tryddyn Jn. ⊕								7*33	7*45									9* 2
Coed Talon ⊕ dep.			E—Arr. 7.0 p.m.		E—Arr. 7.0 p.m.			7 42	7 54									9 11
Llanfynydd								7 45	7 57									9 14
Ffrith								7 48	8 0									9 17
BRYMBO ⊕ arr.								7 54	8 6									9 23
Llong dep.			6 37		6 37								8 30					
Padeswood & Buckley			6 40		6 40								8 33					
Hope Exchange arr.													8 36					
Hope Exchange dep.			6 43		6 43								8 37					
Hope & Penyffordd			6 46		6 46								8 40					
Kinnerton			6 52		6 52								8 46					
Broughton & Bretton			6 56		6 56								8 50					
Saltney Ferry			7E 1		7E 1								8 54					
Mold Junction No. 1 pass			7X 2		7X 2								8X56			9X 4		
Saltney Junction			7 4		7 4								8 58			9 7		
CHESTER arr.			7 8		7 8								9 2			9 11		
Notes			†—Arrives Llanrhaiadr 5.37.	†—Arrives Llanrhaiadr 5.37 p.m.			One Class only.	One Class only.	One Class only.	†—Arrives 7.16 p.m. Not to run after September 9th.	†—Arrives Llanrhaiadr 7.16 p.m. To commence September 11th.	To commence September 11th. To work 8.32 p.m., Rhyl to Denbigh.	†—Arrives 7.33. Conveys H. & C. traffic from and to stations, Corwen to Denbigh.	Not to run after September 9th.	To commence September 11th.	To run Saturdays only after September 9th. (After working 8.0 p.m. from Brymbo.)	†—Arrives 8.43 p.m.	†—Arrives 8.48 p.m. One Class only.

Station	53	54	55	56	57	58	59	60	61	62	63	64	65	66	67	68	69
	PASSENGER.	PASSENGER.	Empty Stock.	PASSENGER.	PASSENGER.	PASSENGER.	PASSENGER.	PASSENGER.	PASSENGER.	Light Engine.	PASSENGER 10.30 p.m. from Rhyl.	Light Engine.	Empty Stock.	Empty Stock.	Empty Stock.	Empty Stock.	Empty Stock.
	SX	SO	SO	SO	SX	SX	SO	SX	SO	SO	SO	SO	WO	ThO	SO	SO	SO
	p.m.	p.m.	p.m.	p.m.	p.m.	p.m.	p.m.	p.m.	p.m.	p.m.	p.m.	p.m.	p.m.	p.m.	night	p.m.	night
CORWEN ⊕ dep.			8 50			9 20			10 20				11 15			11 35	
Gwyddelwern ⊕ arr.																	
Gwyddelwern ⊕ dep.			8*57			9 27			10 27				11*22			11*42	
Derwen						9 32			10 32								
Nantclwyd ⊕ arr.																	
Nantclwyd ⊕ dep.			9* 7			9 38			10 38				11*32			11*52	
Eyarth						9 45			10 45								
Ruthin ⊕ arr.			9*15			9 48			10 48				11 40				
Ruthin ⊕ dep.			9*21			9 50	10 0	10 35	10 50			11 22	11†50	11 57		12* 0	12 14
Rhewl						9 54	10 4	10 39	10 54								
Llanrhaiadr						10† 0	10†10	10†45	11 0								
DENBIGH ⊕ arr.			9 34			10A 8	10 15	10 51	11† 5			11 35	12† 4	12 10		12 13	12 27
DENBIGH ⊕ dep.	9 30	9 30		9 35	9 40						11 10				12 25		
Denbigh Junction ⊕	9 33	9 33		9*38	9*43						11 13				12*28		
Trefnant ⊕ arr.				9 42	9 47												
Trefnant ⊕ dep.				9 43	9 50										12*33		
St. Asaph ⊕ arr.				9 48	9 55												
St. Asaph ⊕ dep.				9 49	9 56										12*38		
Rhuddlan ⊕				9 55	10 1										12*44		
Foryd Junction ⊕				10* 0	10* 5										12*53		
RHYL arr.				10† 2	10† 7										12 56		
Bedfari dep.	9 38	9 38									11 18						
Caerwys	9 45	9 45					Light Engine.	Empty Stock.	PASSENGER.		11 25					Empty Stock.	
Nannerch	9 53	9 53									11 33						
Star Crossing																	
Rhydymwyn	10 0	10 0					WO	SO	SO		11 40					SO	
MOLD arr.	10 5	10 5					p.m.	p.m.	p.m.		11 45					night	
MOLD dep.		10 6					10† 5	10 25	10 30	11 30	11 50					12 45	
Tryddyn Jn. ⊕									10*32		11*52						
Coed Talon ⊕ dep.									10 41		12 1						
Llanfynydd									10 44		12 4						
Ffrith									10 47		12 7						
BRYMBO ⊕ arr.									10 53		12 13						
Llong dep.																	
Padeswood & Buckley		1011															
Hope Exchange arr.																	
Hope Exchange dep.																	
Hope & Penyffordd		1015½															
Kinnerton																	
Broughton & Bretton		1023½															
Saltney Ferry																	
Mold Junction No. 1 pass		10X27					10X25	10X48		11X55						1X10	
Saltney Junction		1029					10 28	10 50		11 58						1 12	
CHESTER arr.		1033					10 33	10 54		12 4						1 19	
Notes	Not to run after September 8th.			†—Public Bills 10.5 p.m.	†—Public Bills 10.0 p.m.	†—Arrives 9.58 p.m.	†—Arrives 10.8 p.m.	†—Arrives 10.43 p.m.	†—Public Bills 11.12 p.m. One Class only.	After working 11.0 p.m. from Brymbo.	One Class only from Mold.	After working 9.38 p.m. from Chester.	†—Light Engine. Not to run after September 6th.		Arrives Foryd Jn. 12*49 a.m.		

A—Two minutes allowed to run through loop at Denbigh.

322

CHESTER, COED TALON, BRYMBO, MOLD, RHYL, DENBIGH, AND CORWEN.

WEEKDAYS.

Miles.			1	2	3	4	5	6	7	8	9	10	11	12	13	14	15	16	17
			MOTOR TRAIN.	PASSENGER.	PASSENGER.	PASSENGER.	MOTOR TRAIN (SX), PASSENGER (SO).	PASSENGER.	PASSENGER.	PASSENGER.	PASSENGER.	PASSENGER.	MOTOR TRAIN.	PASSENGER.	PASSENGER.	PASSENGER.	PASSENGER.	PASSENGER.	PASSENGER.
															SX	SO			SX
			a.m.	a.m.	a.m.	a.m.	a.m.	a.m.	a.m.	a.m.	a.m.	a.m.	a.m.	a.m.	a.m.	a.m.	a.m.	a.m.	a.m.
		CHESTER dep.						6 35	7 34					9 0				10 25	
2		Saltney Junction pass						6 39	7 38					9 4				10 29	
3¼		Mold Junction No. 1						6X41	7X40					9X 6				10X31	
		Saltney Ferry dep.						6 42	7 41					9 7				10 32	
4¾		Broughton & Bretton						6 45½	7 44½					9 11				10 36	
6¼		Kinnerton							7 49					9 16				10 41	
9		Hope & Penyffordd						6 57	7 58½					9 26				10 51	
9¾		Hope Exchange arr.						6 59	8 0½									10 53	
		Hope Exchange dep.						7 0	8 1									10 54	
10¾		Padeswood & Buckley						7 3	8 3½					9 31				10 57	
11½		Llong						7 6	8 6					9 34				11 0	
		BRYMBO (G.W.) ⊕ dep.										8 28					10 0		
	1½	Ffrith										8 33					10 5		
	2½	Llanyfynydd										8 36					10 8		
	4	Coed Talon ⊕										8 40					10 12		
	8¼	Tryddyn Junction ⊕										8*47					10*19		
13¼	8¾	MOLD arr.						7 9	8 9			8 49		9 37			10 21	11 3	
		MOLD dep.							8 11				9 10	9 39				11 5	
16¼		Rhydymwyn							8 17				9 16	9 45				11 11	
18¼		Star Crossing											9 22	9 51					
19¾		Nannerch							8 25				9 25	9 54				11 19	
23		Caerwys							8 31				9 31	10 0				11 25	
25½		Bodfari arr.							8 35				9 35	10 4				11 29	
		Bodfari dep.							8 37				9 37	10 7				11 31	
		RHYL dep.	5 20				7 28			8 30	8 55				9 47	9 50	11 0		11 50
	1	Foryd Junction ⊕	5*23				7*31			8*33	8*58				9*50	9*53	11* 3		11*53
	3½	Rhuddlan ⊕ dep.	5 28				7 36			8 38	9 3				9 55	9 58	11 8		11 58
	5¾	St. Asaph ⊕ arr.	5 33				7 41			8 43	9 8				10 0	10 3	11 13		12 3
		St. Asaph ⊕ dep.	5 34				7†42			8 44	9 15				10 6	10 6	11 14		12 6
	8¼	Trefnant ⊕ arr.	5 39				7†47			8 49	9 20				10 11	10 11	11 19		12 11
		Trefnant ⊕ dep.	5 41				7†50			8 51	9 22				10 13	10 13	11 21		12 14
28¼	10	Denbigh Junction ⊕	5*45				7*54	a.m.	8 41	8*55	9*26		9 41	10 11	10*17	10*17	11*25	11 35	12*18
29¼	11	DENBIGH ⊕ arr.	5 48				7†57		8 44	8 58	9 29		9 44	10 14	10 20	10 20	11 28	11 38	12 21
		DENBIGH ⊕ dep.		6 5	6 43	7 40		8 24	9 5					10†25	10 25	10 25		11 50	
32¼		Llanrhaiadr			6 49	7 46		8 30	9 11					10†31	10 31	10 31		11 56	
34¼		Rhewl			6 54	7 51		8 35	9 16					10†36	10 36	10 36		12 1	
36		Ruthin ⊕ arr.		6 16	6 57	7 54		8 38	9 19					10†39	10 39	10 39		12 4	
		Ruthin ⊕ dep.			7 2				9 21									12 7	
37½		Eyarth			7 8				9 27									12 13	
40¼		Nantclwyd ⊕ arr.			7 15				9 33									12 20	
		Nantclwyd ⊕ dep.			7 21				9 34									12 21	
42¼		Derwen			7 27				9 39									12 27	
45¼		Gwyddelwern ⊕ arr.			7 33				9 45									12 33	
		Gwyddelwern ⊕ dep.			7 38				9 47									12 35	
48		CORWEN ⊕ arr.			7 45				9 53									12 42	
		Notes	One Class only.				One Class only. †—3 minutes later on Saturdays.	PASSENGER.				One Class only.	One Class only.	†—Commences September 11th.	Not to run after September 8th.	To terminate at Denbigh on September 16th and 23rd.	One Class only. PASSGR.		Not to run after September 8th.

	18	19	20	21	22	23	24	25	26	27	28	29	30	31	32	33	34
	PASSENGER.	PASSENGER.	PASSENGER.	PASSENGER.	PASSENGER.	PASSENGER.	PASSENGER.	PASSENGER.	PASSENGER.	PASSENGER.	PASSENGER.	PASSENGER.	PASSENGER.	PASSENGER.	PASSENGER.	PASSENGER.	PASSENGER.
	SO			SO	SO		SO	SX	SO	SX		SX	SO		SX	SO	SX
	a.m.	p.m.	p.m.	p.m.	p.m.	p.m.	p.m.	p.m.	p.m.	p.m.	p.m.	p.m.	p.m.	p.m.	p.m.	p.m.	p.m.
CHESTER dep.			12 10			1 18			2 18	2 25		3†35	3†32		4 25	4 25	
Saltney Junction pass			12 14			1 22			2 22	2 29		3 39	3 36		4 29	4 29	
Mold Junction No. 1			12X16			1X24			2X24	2X31		3X41	3X38		4X31	4X31	
Saltney Ferry dep.			12 17			1 25			2 25	2 32		3 42	3 41		4 32	4 32	
Broughton & Bretton			12 21			1 29			2 29	2 36		3 46	3 46		4 36	4 36	
Kinnerton			12 26			1 34			2 34	2 41		3 51	3 51		4 41	4 41	
Hope & Penyffordd			12 34			1 44			2 44	2 51		3 59	3 59		4 51	4 51	
Hope Exchange arr.			12 36			1 46									4 53	4 53	
Hope Exchange dep.			12 37			1 47									4 56	4 56	
Padeswood & Buckley			12 40			1 50			2 48	2 55		4 4	4 4		4 59	4 59	
Llong			12 43			1 53			2 51	2 58		4 7	4 7		5 2	5 2	
BRYMBO (G.W.) ⊕ dep.				12 55			2 0	2 15									5 0
Ffrith				1 0			2 5	2 20									5 5
Llanyfynydd				1 3			2 8	2 23									5 8
Coed Talon ⊕				1 7			2 12	2 27									5 12
Tryddyn Junction ⊕				1*14			2*19	2*34									5*19
MOLD arr.			12 46	1 16		1 56	2 21	2 36	2 54	3 1		4 10	4 10		5 5	5 5	5 21
MOLD dep.			12 49			1 58			2 56	3 3		4 12	4 12		5 7		
Rhydymwyn			12 55			2 4			3 1	3 8		4 18	4 18		5 13		
Star Crossing			1 1									4 24	4 24				
Nannerch			1 4			2 12			3 9	3 16		4 27	4 27		5 21		
Caerwys			1 10			2 18			3 15	3 22		4 33	4 33		5 27		
Bodfari arr.			1 14			2 22			3 19	3 26		4 38	4 38		5 31		
Bodfari dep.			1 15			2 24			3 21	3 28		4 40	4 40		5 33		
RHYL dep.	11 50			1 18	1†30			2†25			3 20			4 25			5†20
Foryd Junction ⊕	11*53			1*21	1*33			2*28			3*23			4*28			5*23
Rhuddlan ⊕ dep.	11 58			1 26	1 38			2 33			3 28			4 33			5 28
St. Asaph ⊕ arr.	12 3			1 31	1 43			2 38			3 33			4 38			5 33
St. Asaph ⊕ dep.	12 6			1†34	1 48			2 39			3 34			4 39			5 34
Trefnant ⊕ arr.	12 11			1 39	1 53			2 44			3 39			4 44			5 39
Trefnant ⊕ dep.	12 14			1 41	1 55			2 49			3 41			4 46			5 41
Denbigh Junction ⊕	12*18		1 19	1*45	1*59	2 28		2*53	3 25	3 32	3*45	4 44	4 44	4*50	5 37		5*45
DENBIGH ⊕ arr.	12 21		1 22	1 48	2 2	2 31		2 56	3 28	3 35	3 48	4 47	4 47	4 53	5 40		5 48
DENBIGH ⊕ dep.		12 37						3 0	3 41	3 41				5 12			
Llanrhaiadr		12 43						3 6	3 47	3 47				5 18			
Rhewl		12 48						3 11	3 52	3 52				5 23			
Ruthin ⊕ arr.		12 51						3 14	3 55	3 55				5 26			
Ruthin ⊕ dep.									4 6	4 6				5 30			
Eyarth									4 12	4 12				5 36			
Nantclwyd ⊕ arr.									4 18	4 18				5 43			
Nantclwyd ⊕ dep.									4 19	4 19				5 44			
Derwen									4 24½	4 24½				5 50			
Gwyddelwern ⊕ arr.									4 30½	4 30½				5 56			
Gwyddelwern ⊕ dep.									4 31½	4 31½				5†57			
CORWEN ⊕ arr.									4 38	4 38				6† 7			
Notes			One Class only.	PASSGR. SX p.m. †—Public Bills 1.32 p.m.	†—Public Bills 1.28 p.m.		One Class only.	One Class only. PASSGR. p.m. †—Public Bills 2.20 p.m.				†—Public Bills 3.30 p.m. One Class only.	†—Public Bills 3.30 p.m. One Class only.	†—3 minutes recovery time, Gwyddelwern to Corwen.			One Class only. PASSGR. †—P.B. 5.15 p.m. p.m. To run daily until September 9th, then Saturdays only.

Brymbo Branch—Passenger trains cannot cross at Coed Talon.
Vale of Clwyd Branch—Passenger trains cannot cross at Rhuddlan.
Corwen Branch—Passenger trains cannot cross at Nantclwyd or Gwyddelwern.

Rhyl to Denbigh Trains allowed 2 minutes at Trefnant for collection of tickets.
A—Two minutes allowed to run through loop at Denbigh.

323

324

CHESTER, COED TALON, BRYMBO, MOLD, RHYL, DENBIGH, AND CORWEN.

WEEKDAYS—continued.

	35	36	37	38	39	40	41	42	43	44	45	46	47	48	49	50	51	52
	PASSENGER to Rhyl.	PASSENGER.	PASSENGER.	PASSENGER.	PASSENGER.	PASSENGER.	PASSENGER.	Empty Stock.	PASSENGER.	PASSENGER.	PASSENGER.	PASSENGER.	PASSENGER.	PASSENGER.	PASSENGER.	PASSENGER.	PASSENGER.	PASSENGER.
	SO		SO	SX	SX	SO		SO	SX	SO	SX	SO	SX	SO	SX	SO	SX	SO
	p.m.	p.m.	p.m.	p.m.	p.m.	p.m.	p.m.	p.m.	p.m.	p.m.	p.m.	p.m.	p.m.	p.m.	p.m.	p.m.	p.m.	p.m.
CHESTER dep.		5 15			6 5	6 18			6 50	7 0					8 3			8 12
Saltney Junction pass		5 19			6 9	6 22			6 54	7 4					8 7			8 16
Mold Junction No. 1		5X21			6X11	6X24			6X56	7X 6					8X 9			8X18
Saltney Ferry dep.		5 22			6 12	6 25			6 57	7 7					8 10			8 19
Broughton & Bretton		5 26			6 16	6 29			7 1	7 11					8 14			8 23
Kinnerton		5 30			6 21	6 34			7 6	7 16					8 19			8 29
Hope & Penyffordd		5 40			6 29	6 42			7 16	7 26					8 29			8 40
Hope Exchange arr.					6 32	6 45			7 18	7 28					8 31			8 42
Hope Exchange dep.					6 33	6 46			7 19	7 29					8 32			8 43
Padeswood & Buckley		5 44			6 36	6 49			7 22	7 32					8 35			8 47
Llong		5 48			6 39	6 52			7 25	7 35					8 38			8 50
BRYMBO (G.W.) ⊕ dep.	4 55												8 0	8 15				
Ffrith	5 0												8 5	8 20				
Llanyfynydd	5 3												8 8	8 23				
Coed Talon ⊕	5 7												8 12	8 27				
Tryddyn Junction ⊕	5*14												8*19	8*34				
MOLD arr.	5 16	5 51			6 42	6 55			7 28	7 38			8 21	8 36	8 41			8 53
MOLD dep.	5 25	5 53			6 44	6 57			7 30	7 40					8 43			8 55
Rhydymwyn	5 31	5 59			6 50	7 3			7 36	7 46					8 49			9 1
Star Crossing																		
Nannerch	5 39	6 7			6 58	7 11			7 44	7 54					8 57			9 9
Caerwys	5 45	6 13			7 4	7 17			7 50	8 0					9 3			9 15
Bodfari arr.	5 49	6 17			7 8	7 21			7 54	8 4					9 7			9 19
Bodfari dep.	5 51	6 19			7 10	7 23			7 56	8 6					9 9			9 21
RHYL dep.			6 0	6 12			7† 9	7 20			8†32	8 30				8†55	9 0	
Foryd Junction ⊕			6* 3	6*15			7*12	7*23			8*35	8*34				8*58	9* 3	
Rhuddlan ⊕ dep.			6 8	6 20			7 17	7*28			8 40	8 39				9 3	9 8	
St. Asaph ⊕ arr.			6 14	6 25			7 22				8 45	8 44				9 8	9 13	
St. Asaph ⊕ dep.			6 16	6 26			7 23	7*33			8 46	8 45				9 9	9 14	
Trefnant ⊕ arr.			6 21	6 31			7 28	7*39			8 51	8 50				9 14	9 19	
Trefnant ⊕ dep.			6 24	6 33			7 31	7*51			8 53	8 53				9 16	9 21	
Denbigh Junction ⊕	5 55	6 23	6*28	6*37	7 14	7 27	7*35	7*55	8 0	8 10	8*57	8*57			9 14	9*20	9*25	9 26
DENBIGH ⊕ arr.	5 58	6 26	6 31	6 40	7 17	7 30	7 38	7 59	8 3	8 13	9 0	9 0			9†17	9 23	9 28	9 29
DENBIGH ⊕ dep.			6 41	6 41			7 50		8 10	8 15		9 5			9E30	9 35	9 30	9†35
Llanrhaiadr			6 47	6 47			7 56		8 16	8 21		9 11			9E35	9 41	9 35	9†41
Rhewl			6 52	6 52			8 1		8 21	8 26		9 16			9E39	9 46	9 39	9†46
Ruthin ⊕ arr.			6 55	6 55			8 4		8 24	8 29		9 19			9E42	9 49	9 42	9†49
Ruthin ⊕ dep.							8 5					9 20						
Eyarth							8 11					9 26						
Nantclwyd ⊕ arr.							8 18					9 33						
Nantclwyd ⊕ dep.							8 19					9 34						
Derwen							8 25					9 40						
Gwyddelwern ⊕ arr.							8 31					9 46						
Gwyddelwern ⊕ dep.							8 32					9 47						
CORWEN ⊕ arr.							8 39					9 54						
Notes	One Class only to Mold. Denbigh dep. 6.12 p.m.						†—Public Bills 7.5 p.m.	Not to run after September 9th.			†—Public Bills 8.30 p.m.		One Class only.	One Class only.	†—Bay Platform. E—Commences September 11th.	Not to run after September 9th. †—Public Bills 8.52 p.m.	Not to run after September 8th.	†—Commences September 16th.

	53	54	55	56	57	58	59	60	61	62	63	64	65	66	67	68	69
	PASSENGER.	PASSENGER.	PASSENGER.	PASSENGER.	PASSENGER.	PASSENGER.	PASSENGER.	Empty Stock.	PASSENGER.	PASSENGER.	PASSENGER to Brymbo.	PASSENGER.	PASSENGER.	PASSENGER.	PASSENGER.	PASSENGER.	PASSENGER.
	W SX	WO	SO	W SO	SO	SO	SX	SX	SO	SX	SO	Th SX	Th SO	SO	SO	SO	SO
	p.m.	p.m.	p.m.	p.m.	p.m.	p.m.	p.m.	p.m.	p.m.	p.m.	p.m.	p.m.	p.m.	p.m.	p.m.	p.m.	p.m.
CHESTER dep.						9 20	9 25		9†38							11 0	11 48
Saltney Junction pass						9 24	9 29		9 42							11 4	11 52
Mold Junction No. 1						9X26	9X31		9X44							11X 6	11X54
Saltney Ferry dep.						9 28	9 32		9 46							11 7	11 55
Broughton & Bretton						9 33	9 36		9 51							11 12	12 0
Kinnerton						9 39	9 41		9 56							11 18	12 6
Hope & Penyffordd						9 50	9 51		10 6							11 29	12 17
Hope Exchange arr.						9 53	9 53		10 8								
Hope Exchange dep.						9 54	9 54		10 9								
Padeswood & Buckley						9 58	9 57		10 13							11 36	12 24
Llong						10 1	10 0		10 16							11 39	12 27
BRYMBO (G.W.) ⊕ dep.				9 35										11 0			
Ffrith				9 40										11 5			
Llanyfynydd				9 43										11 8			
Coed Talon ⊕				9 47										11 12			
Tryddyn Junction ⊕				9*54										11*19			
MOLD arr.				9 56		10 5	10 3		10 19					11 21		11 42	12 30
MOLD dep.							10 5	10 20	10 21							11 45	12 33
Rhydymwyn							10 11		10 27							11 51	12 39
Star Crossing																	
Nannerch							10 19		10 34							11 59	12 47
Caerwys							10 25		10 40							12 5	12 53
Bodfari arr.							10 29		10 44							12 9	12 57
Bodfari dep.							10 31		10 46							12 11	12 59
RHYL dep.	9 30	9 30	9†32		10 0					10 30	10 30	11 0	11 0		11 45		
Foryd Junction ⊕	9*33	9*33	9*33		10* 3					10*33	10*33	11* 3	11* 3		11*48		
Rhuddlan ⊕ dep.	9 38	9 38	9 40		10 8					10 38	10 38	11 8	11 8		11 53		
St. Asaph ⊕ arr.	9 43	9 43	9 45		10 13					10 43	10 43	11 13	11 13		11 58		
St. Asaph ⊕ dep.	9 44	9 44	9 50		10 18					10 44	10 44	11 14	11 14		11 59		
Trefnant ⊕ arr.	9 49	9 49	9 55		10 23					10 49	10 49	11 19	11 19		12 4		
Trefnant ⊕ dep.	9 51	9 51	9 57		10 25					10 51	10 51	11 21	11 21		12 6		
Denbigh Junction ⊕	9*55	9*55	10 *1		10*29		10 35	10 48	10 50	10*55	10*55	11*25	11*25		12*10	12 15	1 3
DENBIGH ⊕ arr.	9 58	9 58	10 4		10 32		10 38	10 52	10 53	10 58	10 58	11 28	11 28		12 13	12 18	1 6
DENBIGH ⊕ dep.	10 15	10 15			10 35				11 6	11E 0			11 36				
Llanrhaiadr	10 21	10 21			10 40				11 11	11E 5			11 42				
Rhewl	10 25	10 25			10 44				11 15	11E 9			11 47				
Ruthin ⊕ arr.	10 28	10 28			10 47				11 18	11E12			11 50				
Ruthin ⊕ dep.		10 30			10 49												
Eyarth		10 36			10 55												
Nantclwyd ⊕ arr.		10 43			11 2												
Nantclwyd ⊕ dep.		10 44			11 3												
Derwen		10 50			11 9												
Gwyddelwern ⊕ arr.		10 56			11 15												
Gwyddelwern ⊕ dep.		10 57			11 16												
CORWEN ⊕ arr.		11 4			11 23												
Notes		To terminate at Ruthin after September 6th.	†—Public Bills 9.30 p.m.	One Class only.				Not to run after September 8th.	†—Public Bills 9.35 p.m.	E—Thursdays only.	Denbigh depart 11.10 p.m.	Not to run after September 8th.		One Class only.			

Rhyl to Denbigh Trains.—Allowed 2 minutes at Trefnant for collection of tickets.
A—2 minutes allowed to run through loop at Denbigh.

CHESTER, COED TALON, BRYMBO, MOLD, RHYL, DENBIGH, and CORWEN. SUNDAYS.

SUNDAYS.	1	2	3	4	5	6	7	8	9	10	11	12	13	14	15	16	17	18	19
	PASSENGER.	PASSENGER 11.40 a.m. from Chester.	PASSENGER.	PASSENGER 1.25 p.m. from Chester.	PASSENGER.	PASSENGER 4.0 p.m. from Padeswood & Buckley.	PASSENGER.	PASSENGER.	PASSENGER 5.0 p.m. from Rhyl.†	PASSENGER.	PASSENGER.	PASSENGER 7.0 p.m. from Rhyl.	PASSENGER.	PASSENGER 8.40 p.m. from Rhyl.	Light Engine.	PASSENGER.	Light Engine.	PASSENGER 10.30 p.m. from Rhyl.	Empty Stock.
	a.m.	p.m.	p.m.	p.m.	p.m.	p.m.	p.m.	p.m.	p.m.	p.m.	p.m.	p.m.	p.m.	p.m.	p.m.	p.m.	p.m.	p.m.	p.m.
CORWEN ⊕ dep.																			
Gwyddelwern ⊕ arr.																			
Gwyddelwern dep.																			
Derwen																			
Nantclwyd ⊕ arr.	Not to run after September 10th.	Not to run after September 10th.		Not to run after September 10th.		Not to run after September 10th.			†—To start from Denbigh on September 17th and 24th.			Not to run after September 10th.	Not to run after September 10th.	Not to run after September 10th.	To commence September 17th.			Will not run after September 10th.	
Nantclwyd dep.																			
Eyarth																			
Ruthin ⊕ arr.																			
Ruthin dep.			1 40		4 0		5 0				6 55					9 25	10 15		11 32
Rhewl																			
Llanrhaiadr			1 47		4 7		5 7				7 2					9 32			
DENBIGH ⊕ arr.			1 53		4 13		5 13				7 8					9 38	10 28		11 47
DENBIGH dep.	9 32	12 50	1 58	2 40		4 40		5 20	5 45	6 0	7 10	7 45	8 55	9 20	9 30	9 48		11† 7	
Denbigh Junction ⊕	9 35	12*53	2* 1	2*43		4*43		5*23	5 48	6* 3	7*13	7 48	8*58	9 23	9*33	9*51		11 10	
Trefnant ⊕ arr.		12 57	2 5	2 47				5 27		6 7	7 17		9 2			9 55			
Trefnant dep.		12 58	2 7	2 52		4*47		5 28		6 8	7 22		9 3		9*38	9 58			
St. Asaph ⊕ arr.		1 3	2 12	2 57				5 33		6 13	7 27		9 8			10 1			
St. Asaph dep.		1 5	2 14	2 59		4*52		5 35		6 14	7 28		9 10		9*43	10 2			
Rhuddlan ⊕		1 10	2 19	3 4		4*55		5 40		6 19	7 33		9 15		9*49	10 7	Not to run after September 10th.	†—Public Bills 11.5 p.m.	
Foryd Junction ⊕		1*14	2*23	3* 9		5* 0		5*44		6*23	7*37		9*19		9*54	10*11			
RHYL arr.		1 16	2 25	3 11		5† 2		5 46		6 25	7 39		9 21		9 57	10 13			
Bodfari dep.					Not to run after September 10th.				5 53			7 53		9 28					Not to run after September 10th.
Caerwys																			
Nannerch			Not to run after September 10th.	Foryd Jn. arrive 3*8 p.m.		†—Public Bills 5.6 p.m.		Starts from Chester at 4.0 p.m. until September 10th inclusive.		Not to run after September 10th.	Not to run after September 10th.					Not to run after September 10th.			
Star Crossing																			
Rhydymwyn	9 55								6 10			8 10		9 45					
MOLD arr.	10 0								6 15			8 15		9 50				11 33	
MOLD dep.	10 4								6 17			8 17		9 52				11 35	Empty Stock.
Tryddyn Jn ⊕																			
Llong dep	10 8								6 21			8 21		9 56					
Padeswood & Buckley	10 11								6 24			8 24		9 59				11 43	
Hope Exchange arr.																			
Hope Exchange dep.																			p.m.
Hope & Penyffordd	10 16								6 29			8 29		10 4				11 48	11 50
Kinnerton																			
Broughton & Bretton																			
Saltney Ferry																			
Mold Junction pass	10X24								6X37			8X37		10X12					12X 2
Saltney Junction	10 26								6 39			8 39		10 14					12 4
CHESTER arr.	10 30								6 43			8 43		10 18					12 8

SUNDAYS.	1	2	3	4	5	6	7	8	9	10	11	12	13	14	15	16	17	18
	Empty Stock	PASSENGER to Rhyl.	PASSENGER.	PASSENGER to Rhyl.	PASSENGER	PASSENGER.	PASSENGER to Rhyl.	PASSENGER to Rhyl.	PASSENGER to Chester.	PASSENGER.	PASSENGER to Chester.	PASSENGER.		PASSENGER to Chester.	PASSENGER.	PASSENGER to Hope & Penyffordd	PASSENGER.	PASSENGER.
	a.m.	a.m.	p.m.	p.m.	p.m.	p.m.	p.m.	p.m.	p.m.	p.m.	p.m.	p.m.		p.m.	p.m.	p.m.	p.m.	p.m.
CHESTER dep.		11 40		1 25			3‡20	4 0										10 15
Saltney Junction pass		11 44		1 29			3 25	4 4										10 19
Mold Junction		11X46		1X31			3X27	4X 6										10X21
Saltney Ferry dep.																		
Broughton & Bretton							Arrives Padeswood 3‡48 p.m.											
Kinnerton																		
Hope & Penyffordd		12 0		1 45				4 20			†—Public Bills 6.55 p.m.							10 35
Hope Exchange arr.																		
Hope Exchange dep.																		
Padeswood & Buckley		12 6		1 51			4 0	4 26										10 41
Llong		12 9		1 54				4 29										10 44
BRYMBO (GW) ⊕ dep.	12 20																	
Coed Talon ⊕	12*30																	
Tryddyn Junction ⊕	12*37																	
MOLD arr.	12 39	12 12		1 57			4 5	4 32										10 47
MOLD dep.		12 14		2 0			4 8	4 33										10 49
Rhydymwyn		12 20		2 6				4 39										10 55
Star Crossing			Not to run after September 10th.			Not to run after September 10th.			Not to run after September 10th.	Not to run after September 10th.	Not to run after September 10th.	Not to run after September 10th.		Not to run after September 10th.	Not to run after September 10th.	Not to run after September 10th.		
Nannerch																		
Caerwys																		
Bodfari arr.		12 36		2 22				4 55										11 11
Bodfari dep.		12 37		2 23				4 56										11 12
RHYL dep.			12 40		2 30				5 0	5 45	7† 0	8 0		8 40	9 20	10 30	10 40	
Foryd Junction ⊕			12*43		2*33				5* 3	5*48	7* 3	8* 3		8*43	9*23	10*33	10*43	
Rhuddlan ⊕ dep.			12 48		2 38				5 8	5 53	7 8	8 8		8 48	9 28	10*38	10 48	
St. Asaph ⊕ arr.		Denbigh depart 12.50 p.m.	12 53	Denbigh depart 2.40 p.m.	2 43		Not to run after September 10th.	Denbigh depart 5.20 p.m.	5 13	5 58	7 13	8 13		8 53	9 33		10 53	
St. Asaph dep.			1 4		2 44				5 15	6 0	7 14	8 15		8 55	9 35	10*43	10 54	
Trefnant ⊕ arr.			1 9		2 49				5 20	6 5	7 19	8 20		9 0	9 40		10 59	
Trefnant dep.			1 11		2 51				5 29	6 9	7 21	8 22		9 4	9 41	10*48	11 1	
Denbigh Junction ⊕		12 41	1*15	2 27	2*55		4 30	5 0	5*33	6*13	7*25	8*26		9* 8	9*45	10*52	11* 5	11 16
DENBIGH ⊕ arr.		12 44	1 18	2 30	2 58		4 33	5 3	5 36	6 16	7 28	8 29		9 11	9 49	10 55	11 8	11 19
DENBIGH dep.			1 19		3 0	4 30				6 18		8 45			9 50		11 12	
Llanrhaiadr			1 25		3 6	4 36				6 24		8 51			9 56		11 18	
Rhewl																		
Ruthin ⊕ arr.			1 32		3 13	4 43				6 30		8 57			10 2		11 24	
Ruthin dep.		Not to run after September 10th.		Not to run after September 10th.			Denbigh depart 4.40 p.m.	Not to run after September 10th.	Denbigh depart 5.45 p.m.		Denbigh depart 7.45 p.m.			Denbigh depart 9.20 p.m.		Denbigh depart 11.7 p.m.		
Eyarth																		
Nantclwyd ⊕ arr.																		
Nantclwyd dep.																		
Derwen																		
Gwyddelwern ⊕ arr.																		
Gwyddelwern dep.																		
CORWEN ⊕ arr.																		

12. Denbigh. 25th September 1960. A general view of the station platform and buildings, taken from the track, between the Up & Down Loop and the through platform road. The extent of the canopy can be seen in this view, and gives some protection to passengers whose train arrived or departed from the bay platform, where a two coach non-corridor set stands awaiting the next turn of duty. In the distance, smoke and steam indicate the presence of a locomotive, in this case working a train to Ruthin. *D.S. Foulkes Roberts.*

Denbigh

Denbigh's historical associations extend way back in time, and are sufficiently well documented elsewhere to justify exclusion from this work. It was the establishment of a postal service in October 1572, during the reign of Queen Elizabeth I, to ensure regular communication between the Court and the Lord Lieutenant of Ireland that created the establishment of postal stages for a weekly mail service via Chester and the port of Liverpool. Four years later the route was switched to Holyhead, which included a staging post at Denbigh that initially established the town on a recognised through route. The service was short-lived and was withdrawn in 1582. When it resumed in 1598 the Denbigh stop was superceded by Rhuddlan, but nevertheless the service passed by the town. The Act of Union saw the route changed and followed the inland route along what is now the A 5, avoiding the coast road and the town of Denbigh, although it was the necessity to provide a better and reliable means of travel for the Irish M.P.'s who sat in Westminster, that ultimately led to the commissioning of Telford to survey the route which was completed about 1819. Until the coming of the railway to Denbigh, feeder coaches worked to the town from Corwen, and from St.Asaph on the coast route from Chester to Holyhead. With the opening of the Chester & Holyhead railway, Eli Lewis operated a thrice weekly carrier service to Denbigh from Rhyl.

It was the construction of the Vale of Clwyd Railway, incorporated by an Act of 23rd June 1856, that brought railways to the town, but the background and details of this company will be found in a separate work. Sufficient to say that the line from Foryd Junction to a temporary station at Denbigh was inspected by Captain Ross on 22nd September 1858 and opened to traffic on 5th October. The permanent station at Denbigh opened in December 1860 and was well established by the time the Mold & Denbigh came into operation on 12th September 1869, which completed the junction of the three lines at the station.

The station building was an imposing structure and, according to Gordon Biddle's *Victorian Stations* had a stone frontage, a buttressed tower with low spire. He further suggests that the building might have been built as a school, but no evidence has come to light to support this theory. The stone used was limestone, similar in appearance to the church at Bodelwyddan which is commonly called 'The Marble Church'. In all probability, the limestone used came from Craig, the local limestone quarry, and which was served by the railway. Certainly the building were lavish for a small railway, albeit the headquarters of the line.

There was one main through and one bay platform, the latter facing towards Rhyl and Mold, used mainly by Rhyl trains. Station working presented certain difficulties, particularly after the grouping, when the nominally independent Mold & Denbigh Junction Railway finally became absorbed into the L.M.S. There were the usual facilities of booking hall, general waiting room, ladies waiting room, parcels office and toilets provided on the main through platform face, and a canopy extended over from the building and over the platform to give some protection to passengers, who were exposed to the weather in their elevated position above the town. The canopy extended the length of the building and also gave some cover to part of the bay platform, but did not extend to the platform edge. The exterior of the station faced a courtyard which had limited space for vehicles. The Goods Warehouse protruded into the forecourt and had a single track into the building. A carriage landing ran parallel to the bay platform enabling side or end loading of vehicles. Various store-sheds and offices were added over the years.

The track complex was restricted and platform curved through thirty degrees from the bridge over Vale Street to head north towards Denbigh Junction signalbox. The Goods shed, carriage landing, weigh bridge road, two sorting sidings and a long siding which served the cattle pens were located on the Up side. A private siding line from the Graig Quarry came in on the Up side on a falling gradient, ending in a headshunt, off which a trailing connection to the Up line was made, controlled from No.1 signal box, located opposite the engine shed throat. In the 'V' between the Graig Quarry line and the cattle pen road, a 42ft. diameter turntable was located. This was initially installed as a standard 40ft LNWR pattern but it was replaced by a 42ft diameter model about the turn of the century. This itself was subsequently replaced in 1935 with a 50ft diameter turntable that came from Holyhead, itself replaced by a new 70ft diameter structure. According to Vernon Roberts, who started his railway service at Denbigh, and is currently driving from Chester, the centre pin for the table cracked in March 1955, and was subsequently repaired or replaced. The table remained in use after the shed closed. Mold Junction men turned their engines prior to working back home with one of the daily freight turns. Fowler and Stanier 2-6-0 engines could be accommodated on this table but not the Class 5 4-6-0.

On the Down side heading north, opposite the main station building, a small timber yard was served by a trailing siding off the Up and Down passenger loop line. A release road to and from the shed ran parallel to the running lines. A second release line ran from the shed off which was a siding to the coal merchant's siding and another siding which served the town gasworks. The two road engine shed had access to the Up and Down main lines and through the release roads, converging on the Passenger Loop line in front of the gasworks. Two sidings extended behind the loco shed, on either side of the building, the line between the running lines and the shed wall sometimes being used to store passenger rolling stock. The other line passed behind the shed and divided, one leading to the turntable, the other inclined up a ramp, which was used for hand coaling locomotives. A coal stack and water tank stood a short distance from the shed doors on one of the release roads. A facing siding off this release road led to a second timber yard, along side of which was a raised timber wharf.

Until 1957, three signal boxes controlled traffic movements through the station. Working north from the Ruthin end was Denbigh No.2. cabin - shown in the 1937 Sectional Appendix as Denbigh Platform box but carrying the nameboard 'Denbigh No.2.' - and was a small composite structure that housed the frame which controlled 6 points and 7 signals. Single line block operation through the platform line was in force, together with an additional running line, referred to as the Loop line, between No.2. box and No.1. box. At one time No.1. box was called 'Denbigh Station Box. It was located 281 yards to the north, and situated at the north end of the station on the Up side, between the cattle pen and the sorting roads. This box was also of composite construction, measuring 23ft 0ins by 12ft 0ins. and housing a lever frame which controlled 18 points and 20 signals.

1700 yards north was Mold & Denbigh Junction box, where the lines to Rhyl and Mold diverged. According to the *Temporary Speed Restrictions* Booklet for Saturday 4th May to Friday 10th May 1957 (ERO 19092, W2 - No.18), until Sunday 5th May 1957, this box was in regular use but from that date it '... ceased to be operational and the points and signals taken out of use. The former Up line to Bodfari was slued to connect with the Down line to Denbigh. The former Down line between Mold & Denbigh Junction and the new Denbigh Station box, which came into operation on the same date, now became the Up and Down Chester line and the former Up line between these points became the 'Up and Down' Rhyl line'. On the same date, Nos.1 and 2 boxes were replaced by a new box, known as 'Denbigh Station Box' located between the Loop Line and the Coal Siding, 15 yards on the Ruthin side of the former No.1. box.

In September 1961, Denbigh Station box was open for duty on Mondays to Fridays from 5.10am until 10.30pm, and on Saturdays from 5.10am until 11.25pm. Normally there was no Sunday service, but most track maintenance and renewal work was done on that day, when the section of line was handed over to the District Engineer.

In 1952, The first train of the day ran into the bay platform at Denbigh at 5.49am. This was the 5.20am from Rhyl, which also conveyed Mail. A pair of two-coach sets of coaching stock were stored overnight at Denbigh, parked on the siding adjoining the bay platform line buffing up to the carriage landing. The leading set formed the 5.58am to Rhyl, and with the loco coming off shed, attached itself to the two sets, which it drew forward before setting back onto the through platform line, where the sets were divided. In winter this loco would 'gong off' the shed disc fifteen minutes earlier, in order to heat the carriages. The second engine off shed would run through the loop and set back to attach itself to the second coach set, which formed the 6.05am to Ruthin. Once that had departed, the 5.20am from Rhyl set back and drew forward onto the through platform road, where it formed the 6.25am to Corwen, due there at 7.35am. It returned with the 8.10am before working through to Rhyl. At Denbigh it ran through the loop to clear the stock of the 7.20am from Chester to Corwen, which stood at the south end of the through platform, before setting back into the north end of the through platform road. Meanwhile the goods engine had come off shed about 6.20am to shunt the yard, and make up the daily goods for Corwen, which departed about 9.50am. Stock from the 5.15am from Mold Junction, due 6.45am, was sorted and vehicles attached for working forward to their destination. Rhyl trains normally worked from the bay platform, whilst the Chester bound trains stood at the north end of the main platform. Trains from Chester usually worked through to Corwen, and the procedure adopted was that the Chester working would take the loop line through the station before setting back to the platform face under the watchful eye of the Station Master and the guard.

Even after September 1955, when the Rhyl line passenger train services were withdrawn and most south-bound trains working to

Ruthin, with only one main platform face, there were still operational problems at certain times. The services seemed to be timed to enable trains to be despatched almost simultaneously to Chester and Ruthin.

Examination of the working time tables should clarify the picture. As already mentioned, after closure of the shed, there was quite a lot of light engine working between Rhyl and Denbigh.

Latterly the train services over the line could be hauled by a variety of motive power. The last set of diagrams for the workings were nominally allocated to Stanier versions of the 2-6-4T, with a two coach non corridor set in tow. In practice. though, Hughes/ Fowler 2-6-0 'Crabs', B.R. Standard Class 2 2-6-0's, and the occasional Class 4 tank engines worked the services. The turntable at Denbigh, must have suffered some defect, and was not deemed worth repairing, and tender first running became commonplace. To avoid tender first workings back to Chester, some of the workings were restructured to became three-corner trips. Locomotives were changed at Denbigh, with light engine running to and from Rhyl where they were turned before returning to Chester along the coast.

Following the complete withdrawal of passenger services from 30th April 1962, Denbigh station remained open to parcels and some freight traffic, and mail trains worked between Rhyl and Ruthin for a couple of years, until the facility was withdrawn.

With the demise of steam, the surviving freight workings were generally in the charge of Class 24 Bo-Bo diesels, based at Llandudno Junction, but these workings did not warrant inclusion in the working time table, and were confined to the Chester District Trip Working and Shunting Engine booklets.

The freight traffic was progressively discouraged and strangled, and ultimately withdrawn. The station and shed buildings survived for some time after the tracks were lifted, but ultimately the station building was demolished, although there had been a proposal to have it declared a 'Listed Building'.

13. Denbigh. 26th September 1961. Following the withdrawal of passenger services between Ruthin and Corwen in February 1953, and Denbigh to Rhyl in September 1955, the surviving passenger service operated between Chester and Ruthin, although the other lines remained open for freight traffic. In this view, Ivatt 2-6-2T No.**41276** of Rhyl shed (6K) approaches the bridge over Vale Street towards Denbigh's through platform with a Ruthin to Chester working. Train working through the station on both lines was bi-directional and the lower arm of the bracket signal controls access to the 'Up & Down Loop' line. The Down Starter for Ruthin, complete with its track circuit indicator diamond, had to be located beyond the bridge due to the need to accommodate longer trains which necessitated engines standing off the platform and on the bridge. Notice the enamel station sign on the bridge, now worth a tidy fortune at Railwayana auctions!

D.S. Foulkes Roberts.

14. Denbigh. 30th June 1964. The railway bridge over Vale Street dominated the scene at the lower end of the town. By the time this photograph was taken, the passenger service to Denbigh from Chester had been withdrawn, although the daily freight to Ruthin still ran. The enamel sign affixed to the boarding on the bridge had now been removed and the poster boards under the bridge now displayed non-railway information. Road traffic for Rhyl turned left at the junction, and right for Ruthin and Mold. Notice the variety of cars, a Triumph Herald waiting behind a Morris Minor at the junction, whilst an Austin 'Countryman' saloon heads for Rhyl. The traffic bollards were of traditional pattern, whilst the black & white road signs beyond the bridge have mostly been replaced by their modern equivalent. The freight traffic to Ruthin ceased on 1st March 1965, and eventually the bridge was removed and the abutments cut back. *D.S. Foulkes Roberts.*

15. Denbigh. 30th June 1964. Another view of the railway bridge, this time taken from across the road and looking up Vale Street. The bridge was a substantial structure, carrying two tracks. The name signs on the bridge rails had gone, although the frame that held the sign is still in place. Just visible on the left hand edge of the picture is the Down Starter. Notice the modern fluorescent lamp between the traffic bollards, and the old style 'Low Bridge' sign affixed to it. The road approach to Denbigh passenger station was beyond the parked Standard '9' saloon on the right hand side. Traffic parked on one side of the road, alternating each day, presumably to reduce complaints from residents. *D.S, Foulkes Roberts.*

16. Denbigh. 22nd April 1957. The BR Standard Class 4 2-6-4T were relative strangers on the Chester-Denbigh-Ruthin service, but popular with the traincrews for their comfortable cabs, amongst other things. Here, No.**80086** of Chester shed (6A) stands at the head of a two coach local for Ruthin. Judging by the position of the water column bag, the fireman is topping up the tanks. Notice Denbigh No.2. signal cabin, looking something like a garden shed on a brick plinth. This was replaced when the new Denbigh Station box came into operation six days later, hence the two sets of point rodding shown here, the set in the foreground alongside the Up & Down Loop line coming from the new cabin, and which replaced those on the platform line bridge girder. *W.A. Camwell.*

17. Denbigh. 18th September 1961. A typical station scene for the period. A Chester bound train, hauled by a Fairburn 2-6-4T, pulls into the platform with its train of three suburban coaches. A barrow full of parcels stands ready for loading into the guards van, strategically placed and level with where the guard's compartment will come to rest. Passengers stand about awaiting to board, whilst a porter stands in the doorway ready to assist. The photographer's brother is keeping an eye on the camera and subsequently both boarded the train and recorded several views along the line on this day. Behind the barrow of parcels, a porter has taken the train staff from the fireman, watched by a shunter, with pole sloped under his arm. The train in question was the 9.30am from Ruthin, due out of Denbigh at 9.50am and arrived at Chester at 11.00am. The engine was on Chester Diagram No.8 and was worked out and home by Chester men, Turn 243. Notice the platform floor, of brick setts under the canopy and slab edging. There is an abundance of enamel signs visible whilst the clock illustrates this equipment made by Messrs. Joyce of Whitchurch for the LNWR. Notice also the complete absence of litter.

D.S. Foulkes Roberts.

18. Denbigh. 19th September 1961. Count-down to the withdrawal of the Denbigh to Chester service was taking place, yet there is still plenty of activity. A BR Standard Class 4 4-6-0 stands at the head of the 12.46pm to Chester. The leading vehicle of the two coach set is an ex LNER Thompson steel sided non-corridor brake second, the second coach a standard LMS non corridor composite. The goods yard sidings are full of stock. The Chester driver stands on the platform whilst his fireman stands in the cab door. *D.S. Foulkes Roberts.*

19. Denbigh. 28th August 1961. Taken from the 10.50am Denbigh to Chester train, headed by a Fairburn 2-6-4T and looking north. Two single lines ran parallel from outside Denbigh Station signal box, here hidden behind the van. The four arm bracket signal indicates a clear road for the train. The centre-right arm was for the Rhyl line, whilst the left hand pair of signals were for traffic starting from the bay platform. A BR lorry is loading traffic from the van in the goods yard. Beyond can be seen the embankment which carried the line to Graig Quarry. *D. S. Foulkes Roberts.*

20. Denbigh. 26th September 1961. Even after the passenger services from Denbigh to Rhyl, and Ruthin to Corwen had ceased, congestion still occurred in the through platform and it was necessary for trains from Chester working forward to Ruthin to run through the Up & Down loop line, drawing clear of the Up home signal, before setting back into the platform road. In this view, a BR Standard Class 4 4-6-0, working the 5.15pm from Mold, heads its two coach train past the 5.55pm to Chester prior to setting back into the platform road. Somewhat unusually, the last coach on the Chester train is a corridor coach. In the bay platform, a GWR brake van stands at the tail of the evening freight to Mold Junction, which will depart once the passenger train has cleared Bodfari.

D.S. Foulkes Roberts.

21. Denbigh. 19th June 1959. Any Class 5 locomotive seen at Denbigh was a rarity, particularly so the Stanier 2-6-0 version. Possibly the 2-6-4T normally marked for the job had failed, and No.**42976** of Birkenhead shed was pressed into service. These 6C engines were way off their regular diagram at Denbigh although they were frequently seen on passenger turns on the North Wales coast on summer Saturdays, and were capable performers on passenger turns. Here, the 9.30am from Ruthin pulls into the platform, and after a six minute wait will depart for Mold and Chester. Note the 'Wymans' bookstall under the canopy believed to have been closed some time before passenger services ceased in 1962.

D.S. Foulkes Roberts.

22. Denbigh. 22nd April 1957. This view was taken a week before the new Denbigh Station signal box was commissioned, and shows the new signals, prominently marked to show they were not yet in service. Their predecessors lurk behind. On the Up side is the old Denbigh No.1. signal box. According to the 1910 list describing frames and box life expectancy, this controlled 18 points and 20 signals. Its replacement stood on the Down side.

W.A. Camwell.

23. **Denbigh. 19th May 1961.** A closer look at the imposing station front and tower from the forecourt of Denbigh station. The Station Master, Mr Simmonds, stands proudly in front of the steps to his residence. Until the mid 1960's, it was expected that most station masters would live 'over the shop', and the company owned house was part of the "perks" of the job, although in truth, some of the accommodation left a lot to be desired, and it is believed that the station house interior suffered from rising damp, and was draughty, into the bargain. No doubt the availability of plentiful supplies of coal, both the official allocation, and the occasional lump or two that 'fell off the back of the tender', were also accepted as going with the job. *Norman Jones.*

24. **Denbigh. 5th June 1962.** Despite the withdrawal of passenger services from Denbigh on 30th April 1962, the station remained open for parcels and goods traffic, as this poster proclaims, and was displayed prominently in front of the station, and on the advertising hoardings under the railway bridge, and at other locations in the town. Until the late 1960's, posters such as this were produced by local sign-writers, similar examples being found all over the system. Three mail or parcels trains ran daily between Rhyl and Denbigh or Ruthin immediately following the closure, although these were reduced as alternative methods were found. A daily freight worked from Rhyl but certain types of freight were refused and the service declined until its final withdrawal on 1st January 1968. *D.S. Foulkes Roberts.*

25. **Denbigh. 1953.** The station building at Denbigh was an imposing structure, built for the Vale of Clwyd Railway and which incorporated their Headquarters. It was also briefly the headquarters for the Denbigh, Ruthin & Corwen Railway. There was some speculation that the building had been originally designed as a school, but no conclusive evidence has materialised to support this. It was constructed of local limestone, and presented a clean crisp image to the public, although closer inspection showed up weaknesses. The forecourt was somewhat limited in size, but rarely did it become congested with road vehicles. Unfortunately, it was demolished after the line closed to all traffic. *J. M. Dunn.*

26. Denbigh. 19th May 1961. LMS Standard Class 4F 0-6-0 No.**44493**, based at Mold Junction (6B), stands at the head of passenger stock in the bay siding line at the north end of the station. It would seem that some carriage cleaning is taking place, judging by the open door. It is not clear whether the 4F was on passenger train duties, or merely engaged in shunting. Whilst the class was not unknown on passenger workings at Denbigh, Mold Junction engines usually came up on the second through freight working, and after disposing of its train, spent some time on shed, before working back to Mold Junction in the evening. An ex Midland Railway Class 3F 0-6-0 pauses between shunting duties in the goods yard. *Norman Jones.*

27. Denbigh. 19th May 1961. Ex Midland Railway 0-6-0 No.**43618**, after working the daily goods to Corwen and return, then acts as the goods yard shunter for part of the afternoon prior to working back to Rhyl at the end of the turn. Here it shunts the goods yard on the Up side, making up a train for the evening working to Mold Junction. A lot of the inward freight carried was agricultural produce, with animal feedstuffs, fertilizer and grain predominating. These were usually brought in vans, and unloaded into the stores in front of the general goods warehouse. It was necessary to turn the vans round quickly and these were cleared daily. The shunter walks towards the neck to re-set the points in the yard prior to the next move. *Norman Jones.*

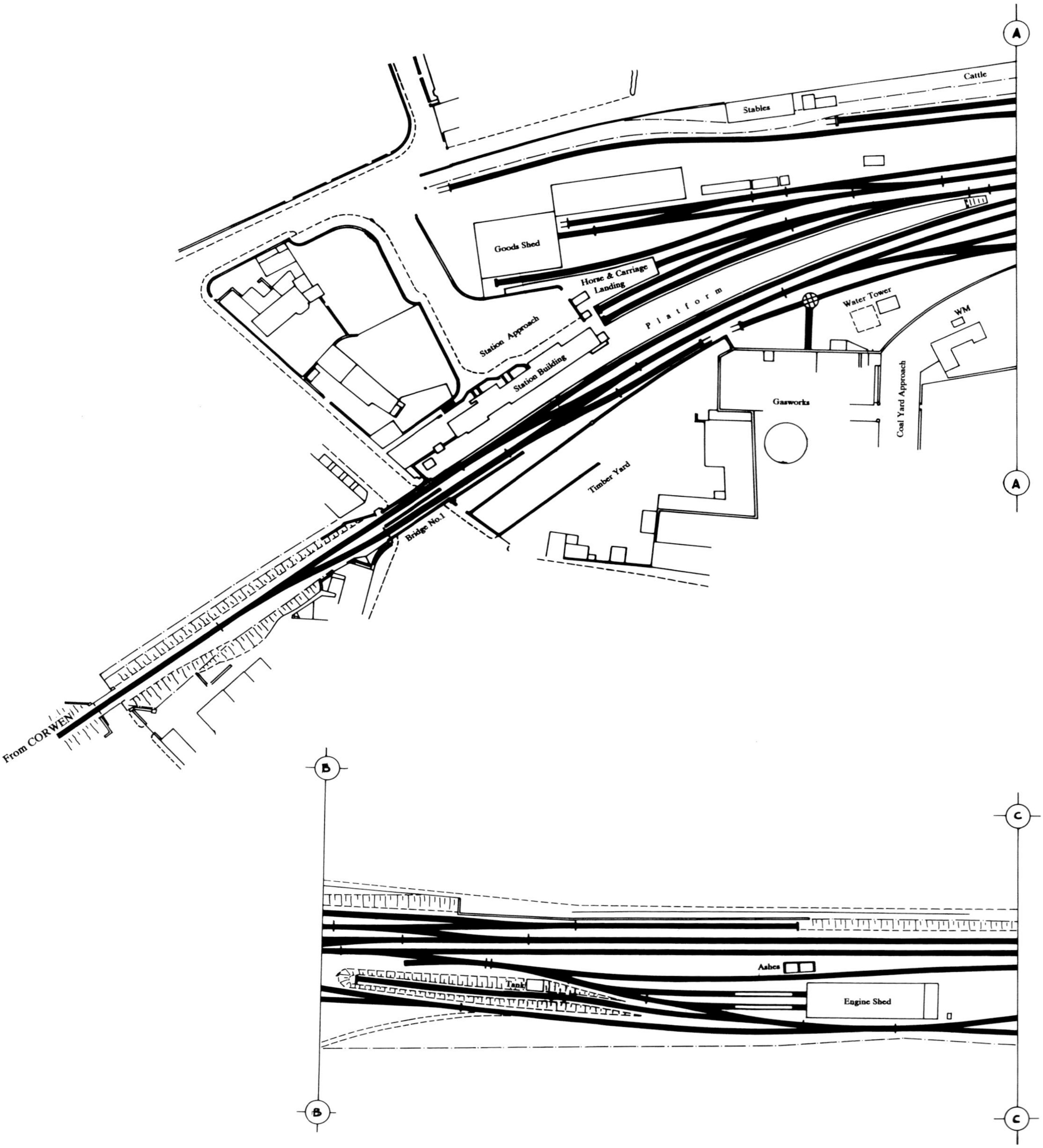
Cattle
Stables
Goods Shed
Horse & Carriage Landing
Platform
Water Tower
WM
Station Approach
Station Building
Gasworks
Coal Yard Approach
Timber Yard
Bridge No.1
From CORWEN
A
B
C
Ashes
Tank
Engine Shed

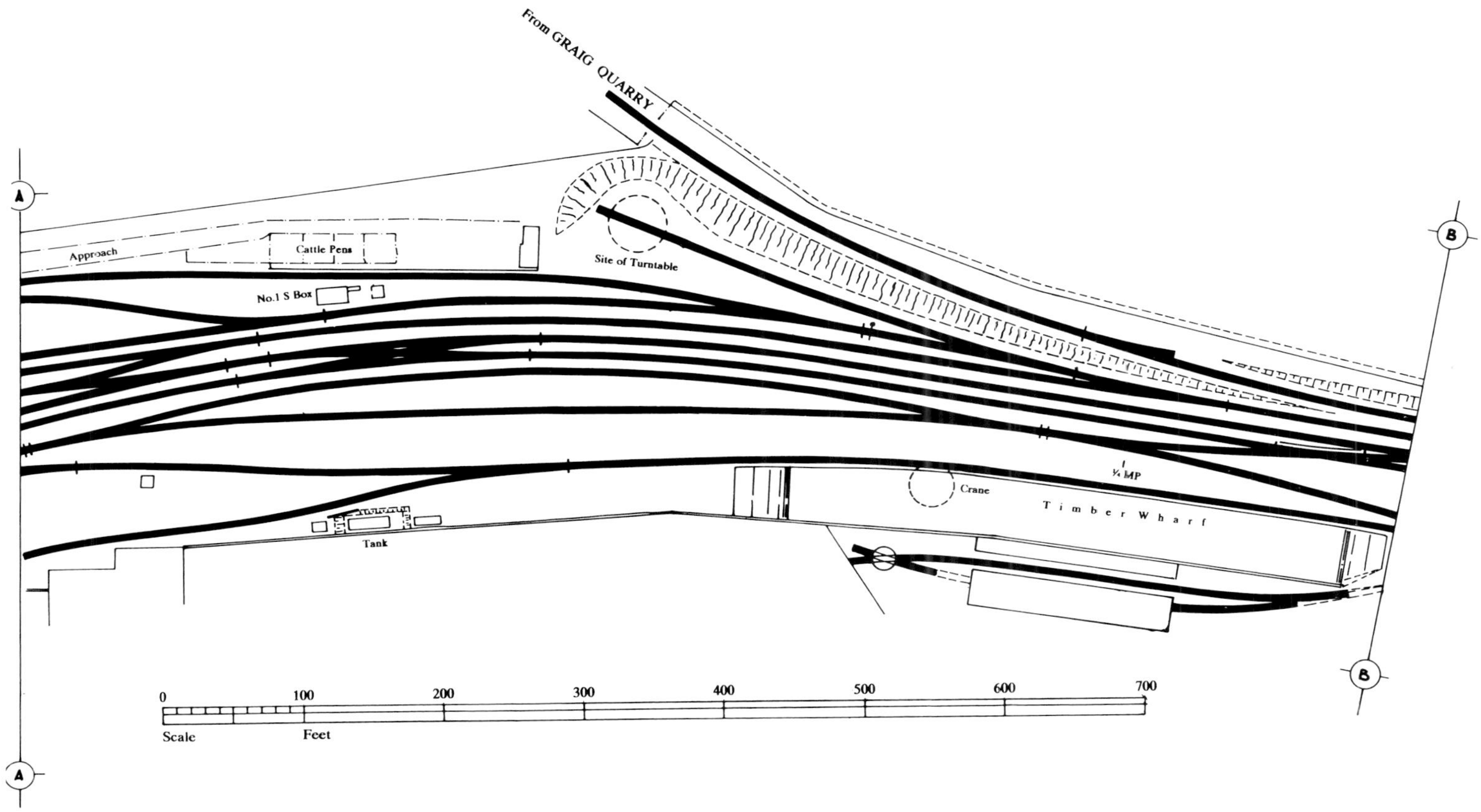
From GRAIG QUARRY
Approach
Cattle Pens
No.1 S Box
Site of Turntable
¼ MP
Crane
Timber Wharf
Tank
0
100
200
300
400
500
600
700
Scale
Feet
A
B

DENBIGH

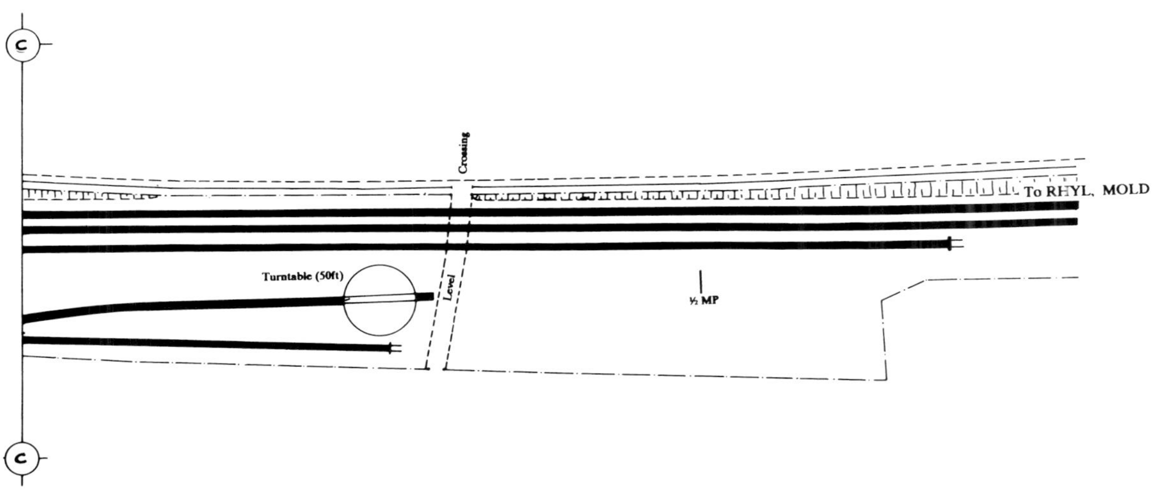
Crossing
Level
To RHYL, MOLD
Turntable (50ft)
½ MP
C

28. Denbigh. 19th May 1961. The station staff at Denbigh pose for their picture outside the station front. Station Master Simmonds is seated in the centre, surrounded by his staff. Unfortunately their names were not recorded, and it is hoped that perhaps some reader will be able to identify them. *Norman Jones.*

29. Denbigh. n.d. Staff at Denbigh station pose for the photographer. The date is early in this century and it would seem that several different grades are present, including the station mascot! Notice the track, the sleepers covered by the ash ballast. *John Dixon collection.*

30. Denbigh. 14th April 1962. The last Station Master to supervise passenger traffic at Denbigh was Mr Thomas, seen here two weeks before all services through Mold to Chester were finally withdrawn. Another Mold Junction Class 4 4-6-0 in the 75xxx series stands at the through platform, with a train for Ruthin. *Norman Jones.*

31.(above) **Denbigh. 19th May 1961.** The Station Master, Mr Simmonds, stands alongside BR Standard Class 4 No.**75054** of Mold Junction (6B) shed, at the head of a Ruthin to Chester train. The 75xxx class were late-comers to the line, and despite the tender first running, were popular with the traincrews. *Norman Jones.*

32. Denbigh. c.1935. A general view of the station building and goods yard, taken from the approximate site of the 1957 replacement signal cabin. There does not appear to be any significant changes from other views of this work, although the most noticeable retention was the two arm lower quadrant starter signals at the north end of the platform, which survived until 1957. In the bay platform, stock for a Rhyl train waits for the engine, whilst a spare coach stands on the bay siding line. In the distance, the roof of Denbigh No.2. signal cabin can just be seen. In the goods yard, an LMS brake van stands on the No.2. siding line. *L.G.R.P.*

33. Denbigh. 10th September 1959. Ex Midland Railway 0-6-0 No.**58287** sets back in the goods yard under the guidance of the shunter, the driver keeping a watchful eye on progress. These engines were coming to the end of their useful life, and the open cab was not always the most comfortable place to be, especially when travelling tender first from Rhyl to take up shunting duties in Denbigh yard. The loco departed for Barrow in the second week of 1960, and its departure, by all accounts, was not mourned by the footplate staff. *Norman Jones.*

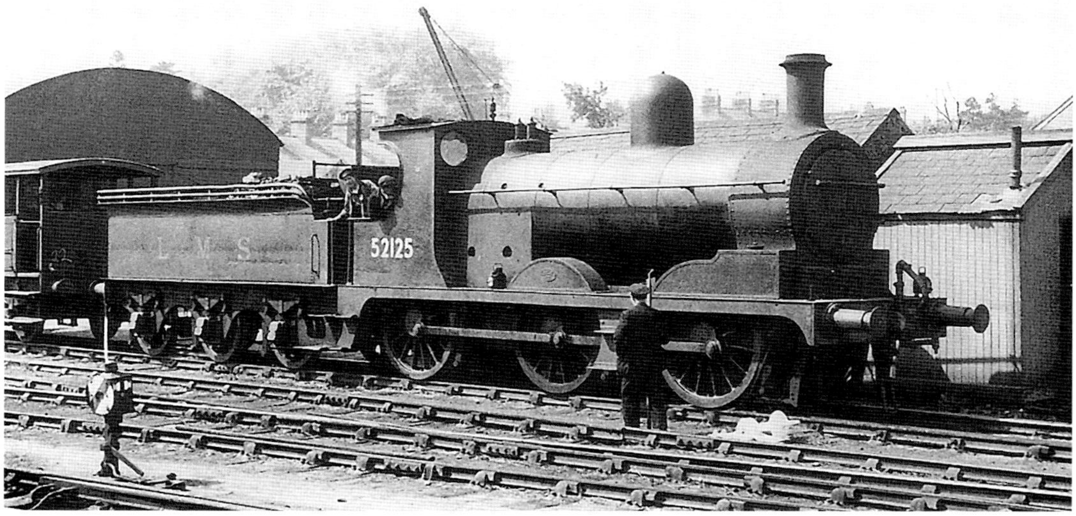

34. Denbigh. 9th May 1949. It was the practice to employ older locomotives on local trip and shunting duties, and in North Wales, both at Bangor and Rhyl, the older LNW engines were replaced by ex L.& Y. Class F19 0-6-0, designed by Aspinall and built between 1889 and 1917. They were powerful engines and whilst not built for the comfort of the train crew, the North Wales allocation were spent on the occasional passenger train working and regularly used for trip work. Here, No.**52125**, formerly LMS No.12125 and L&Y No.1085, not long out of works, sports its new BR number although the overhaul didn't extend to repainting the tender let alone applying the new owner's transfer crest. The amount of freight traffic at this time justified a locomotive engaged on shunting for most of the morning, and the daily Class K freight working from Rhyl shunted the yard before returning home. *Eric S. Russell.*

35. (right) **Denbigh. 19th May 1961.** LMS Class 3F 0-6-0 No. **43618** draws slowly along the Up & Down Loop line to the starter, with the daily 12.55pm (SX) freight to Ruthin, where it would shunt for an hour before working back light engine to Denbigh. There is some activity on the platform, with staff and travellers awaiting the arrival of the 12.25pm passenger from Ruthin to Chester. There was still considerable freight traffic to Ruthin, necessitating this regular working, which cleared Denbigh yard of stock left over by the daily working to Corwen. Provision was made in the freight working time table for a second (conditional) train to work through to Corwen as required, and when this train ran, the loco off the 12.55pm to Ruthin attached on the front of the returned second Corwen working and assisted it back to Denbigh. Notice the gasometer. At one time these structures were prominent landmarks on the skyline throughout the country, but most have now disappeared. *Norman Jones.*

36. Denbigh. 28th August 1961. Taken from a Chester bound train standing at the platform, this view shows the various features on the Down side of the line. Prominent is the water tank, which supplied the columns on the station and also the shed tank. Beyond that is a general store warehouse, constructed after the second World War, and used to house non agricultural stock distributed by private traders. Notice the four arm starting signal, which replaced the two arm lower quadrant starters seen in plate 42. The taller of each pair of signals was for the Rhyl line. *D.S. Foulkes Roberts.*

37. Denbigh. 18th September 1961. The clean modern outline of the replacement Denbigh Station Signal box stand out in this view, as a Chester bound train collects the single line token from the signalman. In the foreground, the Up & Down Loop line starter dominates. Notice the diamond track circuit indicator on the post, very convenient for firemen who would otherwise have to walk to the signal cabin to carry out 'Rule 55', although the distance between signal and box was very short in this instance. The line behind the signal box had to be slued when the new cabin was being built. *D.S. Foulkes Roberts.*

38. Denbigh. 28th August 1961. The coal yard siding at Denbigh was located on the Down side, and extended from the loco shed to the Up & Down Loop line. Road access was off the Denbigh to Rhyl road and the siding was used by several coal merchants who operated from the yard. There was also a release road from the shed that enabled locomotives coming on or off shed to by-pass the platform road. *D.S. Foulkes Roberts.*

39.(top) **Denbigh. 19th September 1961.** At times there was much activity on the platform, and here the 5.10pm from Mold has just pulled into the bay platform, whilst the 5.31pm from Ruthin stands opposite. The two trains were scheduled to arrive within a couple of minutes of each other, which probably gives the impression of an abundance of passengers. The coaching stock on both trains was non corridor, as was usual for the traffic working on the line. Notice the gas lamps along the centre of the platform, the wooden slatted seats and general tidy and presentable appearance of the platform. *D.S. Foulkes Roberts.*

40. Denbigh. 18th September 1961. As the Chester bound train draws out of the platform, a Stanier 2-6-4T stands at the bay starting signal, waiting to draw clear and go on shed for servicing. Notice the grain and agricultural stores, unusually somewhat devoid of stock. An assortment of wagons stand in Nos 1 and 2 sidings. In the goods yard, a crane stands poised for work. *D.S. Foulkes Roberts.*

41. Denbigh. 25th September 1960. Taken from outside the signal cabin, looking towards the station and Ruthin, this view shows the four-arm bracket at the end of the passenger platform and the Up & Down Loop line starter. Notice the point rodding stretching away in the distance. There is some freight stock on view, but generally the yard and sidings were cleared by Saturday night, hence the absence of wagons. This view was one of a series taken through the station by the photographer, and of necessity had to be done on a Sunday. *D.S. Foulkes Roberts.*

42. Denbigh. 25th September 1960. This view depicts the front and side of the replacement Denbigh Station signal box, showing its clean modern functional lines. Behind the box was the release road from the shed, sometimes used for overnight storing of passenger stock. Opposite the box is a ground disc signal, with indicator arrow signifying the relevant line. *D.S. Foulkes Roberts.*

43. (top right) **Denbigh. 19th May 1961.** The replacement Denbigh Station signal box was a considerable improvement on its predecessor, and boasted such modern amenities as electric lighting and an illuminated diagram above the frame. There was less enthusiasm for the standard LMS frame, which was regarded by some as a hernia inducer! Signalmen worked with their back to the line, although their elevated position gave good visibility through the station. Here, signalman A.J.Williams, with his back to the frame, shakes hands with W.O. Hughes, presumably at the shift change-over. The spaciousness of the modern cabin was a distinct improvement on its predecessor, Denbigh No. 1 box. The replacement had a very short life, and was demolished when the station closed to all traffic in 1968. *Norman Jones.*

44.(below) **Denbigh. 10th September 1959.** Signalman W.O. Hughes takes a single line token out of the instrument for the Denbigh to Ruthin section. Three token instruments were located on a cupboard in Denbigh Station box, and were placed with the right hand instrument containing the tokens for the section of line to Ruthin. The left hand, and centrally located instruments, were for the single line sections to Rhyl and Bodfari respectively. *Norman Jones.*

45.(right) **Denbigh. 24th February 1961.** Signalman A.T. Williams stands at the frame of the new Denbigh Station signal box. The frame was a standard LMS 1943 4 " pattern and comprised 70 levers, of which 58 were working. As with the design of boxes for the period, the signalman stood with his back to the traffic, which gave him better visibility to observe trains as they passed, unhindered by the frame and frame diagram blocking his view. The booking desk is located against the front window. In the background can be seen the three token instruments on their stand. The box interior looks immaculate. Most regular signalmen took immense pride in the condition of their box, and part of their routine was to scrub the floor several times each week, shine the lever handles and instruments with metal polish, and keep the windows clean. Most boxes at this time were still illuminated by oil or gas, and heated by coal stoves, and despite the primitive conditions, were a credit to the staff who maintained these high standards. *Norman Jones.*

46. Denbigh. 19th May 1961. Midland Railway Class 3F 0-6-0 No.**43618** sets back with two vans in the Up side sidings making up a freight train for Rhyl. There was one diagram for a 3F at Rhyl, which was used on the daily Corwen freight working. This loco put in a brief appearance at Rhyl in November 1948 when it was on loan from Shrewsbury, but three weeks later it was transferred again to Warrington where it remained for nearly nine years. It was then transferred to Barrow, but was moved to Rhyl in April 1958 and remained there until it was withdrawn in the last week in March 1962. Most of the time it was used on the Corwen freight turn. Notice the remnants of a coach body in use as a store. The shunter rides on the footplate step whilst the fireman sorts out some lumps of coal. The ruins of Denbigh castle dominates the landscape on top of the hill, whilst the town encroaches the surrounding hillside. *Norman Jones.*

47. Denbigh. 12th June 1967. The last regular passenger train had run over five years previously, and Denbigh became the terminal point for a freight only line, connected to the main line near Rhyl. Nevertheless, there was still a considerable amount of freight traffic to and from the yard as this scene shows. The coal siding was still used by the local coal merchants, who distributed to a wide area in the valley, and the daily freight train consisted of several wagons for them. The agricultural produce also provided a steady flow of traffic. Here, Bo-Bo Diesel Class 24 No.**D5072** departs from Denbigh with a train of mixed stock. Like so many other branch lines, this traffic was subsequently strangled, and the line closed. *D.S. Foulkes Roberts.*

48. Denbigh. 28th August 1961. The Motive Power depot closed on 19th September 1955, and the modernised building stood empty for many years, although some servicing of locomotives was done in the yard, locomotives stood on the shed between turns and the turntable, located behind the shed, was still used. The building was demolished some time after the passenger traffic to Chester ceased. Here, a Chester bound train, now on the single line section to Bodfari, passes the shed water tank. Notice the yard lamps and the telephone box on the water tank brickwork. Before locomotives moved off shed, they would telephone the signal box from this point to inform the signalman of their intention. *D.S. Foulkes Roberts.*

49. Denbigh. 7th September 1960. From 1951 until 1961, the Land Cruise trains used to pass through Denbigh station on their circular tour. At their peak, four trains worked the circuit, two in each direction, all starting and terminating in different towns. These were reduced in the final year to one in each direction, and worked the circuit in opposite directions. On this occasion, Standard Class 4 4-6-0 No.**75054**, based for the summer at Rhyl, and transferred to Mold Junction at the end of the season, works the Up 'Welsh Chieftain' Land Cruise, now on the single line section from Denbigh to Rhyl, and is seen passing the shed access road. *D.S. Foulkes Roberts.*

50. Denbigh. 14th July 1961. B.R. Standard Class 4 4-6-0 No.**75053**, of Mold Junction Shed (6B), with the Down 'Cambrian Radio Land Cruise' coasts past the Motive Power Depot, braking gently to the regulation speed of 10 mph to pick up the single line token - for the section to Ruthin - from the signalman outside Denbigh Station signal box before accelerating through the station itself. The leading coach of the formation was formerly a brake first vehicle from one of the 'Coronation' stock sets and one that went to the USA in 1939. It can be identified by the lack of corridor gangway at the brake end. *D.S. Foulkes Roberts.*

51. Denbigh. 25th September 1960. Taken from alongside the motive power depot, looking towards Denbigh station and Ruthin, the parallel single lines are flanked by the shed roads on the left hand side, with the timber yard adjoining, whilst the goods yard line is accessed from the Rhyl line. To the immediate right hand side of the picture, a wagon and van stand on the former Graig Quarry line. Beyond that, at one time, the 42ft turntable was located, but this was subsequently relocated. *D.S. Foulkes Roberts.*

52. Denbigh. 25th September 1960. When the signal box at Mold & Denbigh Junction was taken out of use, the former Down line became the Up & Down Line from Bodfari to Denbigh, whilst the former Up line became the Up & Down Rhyl line. Consequently it was necessary to re-signal the approach to Denbigh station, and these two three-arm bracket signals were installed. *D.S. Foulkes Roberts.*

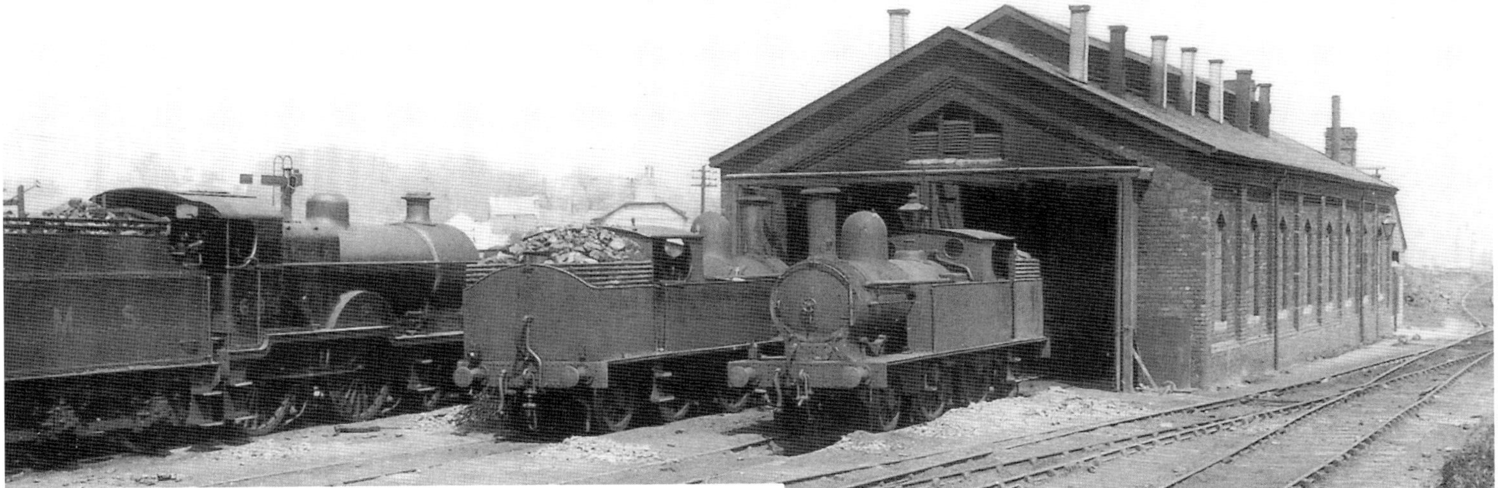

53. Denbigh. 2nd May 1937. The two road engine shed at Denbigh was a traditional LNWR design, listed as 38D and an outpost under Llandudno Junction until the 1933 scheme for 'Motive Power Area Locomotive Supply, Repair, Concentration and Garage Scheme' came into operation, when it became a sub-shed to Rhyl, coded 7D. The building was re-roofed in 1947/8. The allocation in December 1937 consisted of one 4-4-0 (No.**561**), nine 5ft 6ins. 2-4-2T and one ex L&Y 0-6-0 (No.**12428**). Here, the 4-4-0 is No.**695**, with 2-4-2T Nos. **6607** and **6669** standing outside the shed. The converging tracks in the foreground, which passed alongside the shed, led to the 50ft turntable and a coaling ramp. *W.A. Camwell.*

54 (right-centre)**. Denbigh. 11th May 1955.** The Ivatt 2-6-2T engines were familiar sights at three of the North Wales depots, but considered too useful for shunting jobs at Denbigh. Rhyl shed used one on the Holywell Town shuttle and another during summer months on 'The Welsh Dragon', which worked between Rhyl and Llandudno. No.**41232** was attached to Llandudno Junction shed at the time of the photograph, seen here in Denbigh shed yard, with G.V. Williams in the driver's seat and V.L. Roberts on the shovel. *V. Roberts collection.*

55 (above)**. Denbigh. 11th May 1955.** Pictures of Denbigh shed staff are rare, and it is pleasing to include this view, taken in front of Ivatt Class 2 2-6-2T No.**41232**. Standing are H. Roberts, R.E. Edwards, T.G. Jones and R. Ellis, whilst G.V. Williams, V.L. Roberts and J. Jones occupy the front row. *V. Roberts collection.*

56 (opposite)**. Denbigh. 11th May 1955.** Another posed group, this time on the front of Ivatt Class 2 2-6-2T No.**41232**, in front of the shed. In the front row are T. Williams, G.V. Williams, V.L. Roberts and R.E. Edwards, whilst J. Jones, T.G. Jones and R. Ellis cram in, somewhat precariously behind them. It is understood that 'The Black Boys' refer to the cleaning or coaling gang. *V. Roberts collection.*

Engine & Men's Workings.

As previously mentioned, the Mold Railway was worked from the commencement of services by the LNWR, who operated passenger trains from the Mold end, and freight traffic from Chester depot. No details of locomotives specifically allocated to Mold have surfaced, and it must be assumed that former Chester & Holyhead engines might have been used. Similarly few details have emerged about the Mold & Denbigh Junction motive power, and again, the LNWR operated this line from the outset. With the completion of the through route between Chester and Denbigh, Mold shed was closed and work transferred to Chester and Denbigh sheds.

Although Denbigh shed pre-dated both Rhyl and Llandudno Junction, it was always a sub-shed, possibly under Chester following the opening of the Mold & Denbigh Junction line, when the shed at Mold shed and some work was transferred there. When Llandudno Junction became an independent shed (No.38) in 1889, Corwen, Denbigh and Rhyl came under its authority. Denbigh was coded 38D and Rhyl shed, opened about 1870, was coded 38R. When the re-organisation of the Motive Power structure took place in 1935, and Llandudno Junction became the Concentration Depot for the district, Rhyl was given its own code - 7D - and Denbigh became a sub-shed to Rhyl. It thus survived for several years, although playing an increasingly diminishing role, but the loss of the regular passenger services between Denbigh and Corwen from 2nd February 1953, and subsequently the withdrawal of passenger services between Rhyl and Denbigh from 19th September 1955, there was insufficient work to justify its retention as an operational depot, and it was closed on the same date, the work transferring to Rhyl, Mold Junction and Chester, although four duties were retained at Denbigh, the men signing on at the station and the locomotives running light to and from Rhyl. The loss of the passenger service through Mold to Chester on 30th April 1962 saw the Residential Link men disappear, and the limited freight traffic worked on the Vale of Clwyd line as far as Ruthin by Llandudno Junction engines and men. This was cut back to Denbigh on 1st March 1965 until that too was axed on 1st January 1968. The shed building survived the total closure of the line.

The Engine Diagrams for Chester shed for February 1913 have survived, and these show workings to Denbigh and Corwen via Mold attached to No.4 Link, which had 4 sets of men, who worked with two Class 'DX' 0-6-0 and 1 6ft 6ins Passenger engines. The link worked the 6.30am to Corwen through Mold, returning with the 10.30am to Chester. The second 'DX' worked the 8.30am to Denbigh where it shunted, and after turning, returned with the 2.15pm to Chester, due 3.26pm. The loco was re-manned by the second set who worked the 4.07pm to Rhyl, due 5.44pm. They then worked the 6.25pm to Denbigh, due 6.51pm and after turning returning with the 9.00pm through Mold, due Chester at 10.15pm.

First reasonably accurate information about the locomotive stud at Denbigh can be deduced from the photographs taken by the late David Foulkes Roberts, who grew up in Denbigh, and commenced taking photographs from 1917. Most of the passenger workings appeared to be in the hands of 4ft 6ins 2-4-2T and 2-4-0 engines, and the ubiquitous variants of the 0-6-0 classes handling freight work. There were about twenty locomotives based at the shed at this time, which outnumbered the allocation at Rhyl. Recorded on Denbigh shed, and working local services about 1923 were 2-4-0 Precedent Class Nos.**860** *Merrie Carlisle*, **862** *Balmoral*, **1194** *Miranda*, **1520** *Franklyn*, **1666** *Ariadne*, 2-4-2T No.**2219**, 0-6-0 Class 'DX' No.**3002**.

After the General Strike, some work never returned, reflected both in the train services and also in the number of booked turns and engines allocated to Denbigh, which diminished, some work being covered by Rhyl. The work at Corwen was transferred to Denbigh after the GWR shed closed in 1927, but this did little to boost the depot's fortunes. The gradual decline continued and the allocation in 1937 consisted of nine 5ft 6ins 2-4-2T, one Class 2P 4-4-0 and one ex L.& Y. 0-6-0. The outbreak of World War II saw a slight improvement in traffic, particularly freight, after the initial shock of the Emergency Time Table introduced on September 11th 1939, when some passenger services were cut, although the line suffered less than other branches in North Wales. The allocation at Denbigh remained static until after the war, when the reduction in booked jobs continued and by 1952 was down to seven locomotives - four Ivatt 2-6-2T, two Class 2P 4-4-0's and a Class 3F 0-6-0.

The Denbigh staff complement at closure on 19th September 1955 consisted of:

Shed Master:
E. Poynter.

Passenger Drivers:
E. Ellis, E. Evans, D. Jones, E. Jones, W. Jones, R. Johnson, J.L. Roberts, P.L. Roberts.

Freight Drivers:
A. Bowden, E. Pierce.

Shed Drivers:
H. Foulkes, W. Foulkes.

Passed Firemen:
R.E. Edwards, M. Evans, T.O. Jones.

Firemen:
H. Hughes, D.E. Roberts, J.V. Roberts, J. Sullivan, B. Williams, D.G. Williams, G.V. Williams, E. Wynne, K. Wynne.

Passed Cleaners:
L. Jones, T.J. Jones, J. McCabe, R. Morgan, D. Parry, R. Pierce, V.L. Roberts.

In Forces:
C. Lewis, D.L. Roberts.

Fitter:
W. Owen.

Fitter's Mate:
?. Morris.

Steam Raiser:
R. Humphries.

Stores/Water Softener:
J. Royles.

Labourers:
T. Williams, J. Jones.

Coalmen:
I. Jones, J. McKie, H. Roberts.

The withdrawal of passenger services between Chester, Mold and Denbigh, and complete closure from Hendre Siding to Denbigh in 1962 affecting Engine and Enginemen's diagrams and had implications for the following sheds:

Chester.
Locomotive Turn Nos.**8** - 2 2-6-4T, **9** - Class 4 4-6-0, **28** - 2 2-6-4T, **29** - 1 2-6-4T, **30** - 1 2-6-4T, **35** - 1 2-6-4T, **36** - 1 2-6-4T, **39** - 1 2-6-4T, **685** - 1 3F 0-6-0T.
30 Enginemen's Turns.
Mold Junction.
Locomotive Turn Nos:**10** - 3 Class 4 4-6-0, **100** - 1 Class 8F 2-8-0, **105** - 1 Class 8F 2-8-0, **111** - 1 Class 8F 2-8-0, **122** - 2 Class 5 4-6-0, **124** - 2 Class 5 4-6-0, **126** - 2 Class 5 4-6-0, **133** - 1 Class 4F 0-6-0.
18 Enginemen's Turns.
Rhyl.
Locomotive Turn Nos.**2** - 1 Class 2 2-6-0, **4** - 1 Class 2 2-6-0, **19** - 1 Class 2 2-6-2T, **60** - 1 Class 3F 0-6-0, **72** - 1 Class 3F (L.& Y.) 0-6-0.
34 Enginemen's Turns. (4 at Denbigh).
Llandudno Junction.
Locomotive Turn No.**3** - 2 Class 5 4-6-0.
5 Enginemen's Turns.
Crewe North.
2 Enginemen's Turns.
Holyhead.
Locomotive Turn No.**3** - 3 Class 7 (Royal Scot) 4-6-0.
Warrington.
Locomotive Turn No.**5** - 3 Class 5 4-6-0.
1 Engineman's Turn.
Willesden.
Locomotive Turn No.**38** - 2 Class 7P/6F 4-6-0.
Birkenhead.
Locomotive Turn No.**83** - 1 Class 4 2-6-4T.
5 Enginemen's Turns.
Edge Hill.
Locomotive Turn No.**701** - 3 Class 8F 2-8-0.
1 Engineman's Turn.

Examples:

CHESTER
Turn 39.

One Class 4 Tank (ex LMS 2-6-4)

Arr	Station	Dep			
	Chester	5.50am	Pass	SX	(240)
7.44am	Ruthin	7.55	Pass	SX	
9.30	Chester				
9.30	SHUNT (Pass)	10.00		SX	
	Chester	10.40	Pcls.	MSX	
11.32	Birkenhead	12.01pm	L.E.	MSX	
12.38pm	Chester				
	Chester	9.08am	Pass	SO	(6G/122)(231)
9.42am	Birkenhead	11.40	Cpld Pass	SO	
12.38pm	Chester M.P.D.				
	Chester	4.25pm	Pass	D	(279)
5.29pm	Lime Street	7.30	L.E.	SX	
7.44	Edge Hill D.S.	8.15	ECS	SX	
8.23	Lime Street	10.35	Pass	D	
11.35	Chester				
	Chester	10.08am	Pass	Sun	(470)
	(9.10am from Birkenhead)				
12.19pm	Wellington	12.45pm	Pass	Sun	
2.42	Chester				

CHESTER
Turn 243

Arr	Station	Dep			
				a.m.	p.m
				6.45	2.32 7.47
				6.25 S.H.	
	ENGINE PREPARED by Turn 241			SO	
		6.40am	S.H.	SO	
	Chester M.P.D.	7.00	L.E.	SO	
	Chester	7.25	Pass	SO	(8)
9.09am	Ruthin	9.30	Pass	SO	
9.44	Denbigh				
	RELIEF 9.44am for Chester by 6K Turn 123			SO	
	RELIEVE 9.02am from Chester 6K Turn 29 at 10.17am			SO	
	Denbigh	12.46pm	Pass	SO	(28)
1.57pm	Chester	-	L.E.	SO	
2.17	Chester M.P.D.				

MOLD JUNCTION
Turn 111

One Class 8F (STD 2-8-0)

Arr	Station	Dep			
	Mold Jn.	9.23am	Frt	WThFO	(258)
10.19am	Mold				
10.19	SHUNT (Frt)	12.40pm		WThFO	
	Mold	12.40	Frt	WThFO	
1.25pm	Hendre Sidings	1.42	Frt	WThFO	
2.56	Mold				
2.56	SHUNT (Frt)	4.15		WThFO	
	Mold	4.15	Min	WThFO	
5.04	Mold Jn.	5.35	LE	WThFO	(250)
6.63	Saltney	7.05	Frt	WThFO	
7.30	Mold Jn.				
	Mold Jn.	11.30pm	T.F.	TWThO	(292)
1.03am	Ellesmere Port	2.20am	T.F.	WThFO	
3.24	Mold Jn.	-	LE	WThFO	
-	Saltney	4.47	Frt	WThFO	
5.12	Mold Jn.				
	Mold Jn. MPD.	12.18am	LE	SO	(312)(8B/606)
12.30am	Saltney	12.53	EF(FSO	(24L/473)(12F/313)	
	(1.30pm from Llandilo)				
10.31am	Sellafield	-	LE	SO	
-	Workington MPD				
	Workington MPD	3.55am	LE	TO	(12F/312)
4.48am	Sellafield	5.00	EF(F)	TO	
11.34	Saltney	-	LE	TO(24L/514)(8F/708)	
11.54	Mold Jn. MPD.				

MOLD JUNCTION
Turn 256

Arr	Station	Dep			
		a.m.		p.m.	
		5.40		1.40	8.00 SX
		5.40		1.15	7.35 SO
	RELIEVE Freight Shunt Turns 232 and 330 at 6.00am			D	
6.00am	SHUNT (Frt)	6.30am		D	
	Mold Jn.	6.30	T.F.	D	(133)
6.53	Hope & P.	6.58	T.F.	D	
7.13	Mold				
7.15	SHUNT (Frt)	9.00		D	
	Mold	9.00	Min	D	
9.25	Coed Talon	10.15	Min	D	
10.35	Mold	10.50	Frt	D	
12.25pm	Mold Jn				
	RELIEF 1.15pm for 1,45pm Muspratts Sdgs. by Turn 253			SX	
	Mold Jn.	-	LE	SO	
12.45	Mold Jn. MPD.				

RHYL
Turn 60

One Class 3F (Mid. 0-6-0)

Arr.	Location	Dep.			
	Rhyl MPD	6.00am	LE	SX	(34)(6B/244)
6.30am	Denbigh				
6.30	SHUNT (Frt)	8.05		SX	
	Denbigh	8.10	Frt	SX	(121)
8.30	Ruthin				
8.30	SHUNT (Frt)	9.00		SX	
	Ruthin	9.00	Frt	SX	
10.42	Corwen	12.20pm	Frt	SX	
2.15pm	Denbigh				
3.40	SHUNT (Frt)	6.00		SX	(26)
	Denbigh	6.05	LE	SX	
6.30	Rhyl				

DENBIGH
Turn 122

p.m. p.m.
3.00 11.05 8.05

Arr.	Location	Dep.			
	RELIEVE 1.35pm Pass from Chester 6B Turn 40 at 3.10pm				
	Denbigh	3.22pm	Pass	SX	(6B/10)
4.37pm	Chester	6.35	Pass	SX	
8.09	Ruthin	8.25	Pass	SX	
8.39	Denbigh	8.45	ECS	SX	
9.07	Rhyl		LE	SX	
9.22	Rhyl MPD				
	LEAVE ENGINE				
	Rhyl	10.05	By bus	SX	
10.50	Denbigh				

Certain classes of locomotives were prohibited from working over the line, but these were restricted to No.**46170** *British Legion*, the LMS Pacific Classes and BR Class 8P No.**71000** *Duke of Gloucester*, hardly what would expect to see working through Nannerch! Some of the older LM and Southern Region Main Line diesels were likewise restricted,

The London Midland Region Western Division booklet *Loads of Passenger Trains* (BR 31162/3 - issued 1st November 1954) gives the following Maximum Load in Tons for the various permitted classes over the line:

Section of line	Down or Up	Class of Engine 1	2	3	4	5	6
Chester - Hope	Down	95	125	155	170	195	220
Hope - Denbigh	Down	165	225	270	300	345	390
Denbigh - Chester	Up	135	185	225	250	290	325

The loading of freight trains was similarly controlled in the publication *Loads of Freight Trains* (BR 31162/4). The relevant extract for the line for Class '**J**' trains is as follows:

Between	UP MINERAL Class of Engine 2	3	4	5	6	7	8	DOWN MINERAL Class of Engine 2	3	4	5	6	7	8
Denbigh and Hendre Sg	18	22	26	29	31	34	37	24	29	35	38	42	46	51
Hendre & Rhydymwyn	41	49	59	65	71	79	87	24	29	35	38	42	46	51
Rhydm'n & Padeswood	41	49	59	65	71	79	87	34	40	48	53	59	64	70
Padeswood & Hope Jn.	26	32	38	42	46	51	56	34	40	48	53	59	64	70
Hope Jn. & Mold Jn.	26	32	38	42	46	51	56	8	10	12	13	15	16	18
Mold & Coed Talon	18	22	26	29	31	34	37	26	32	38	42	46	51	56

57. Denbigh. 25th November 1961. Following the closure of Denbigh shed in 1955, it was necessary for engines to work to Rhyl shed for servicing. Here, Fairburn Class 4 2-6-4T No.**42213** of Chester L.M. shed (6A) is coupled to Midland Class 3F 0-6-0 No.**43618**, which had worked the daily freight to Corwen and return, scheduled to work light engine back to Rhyl shed. The tank engine had worked a passenger train from Chester to Ruthin before travelling LE to Rhyl. To avoid excessive line occupation, the 4P was coupled in front, and the trailing engine, held the single line token, seen here being delivered by signalman Jones, outside Denbigh signal cabin. *Norman Jones.*

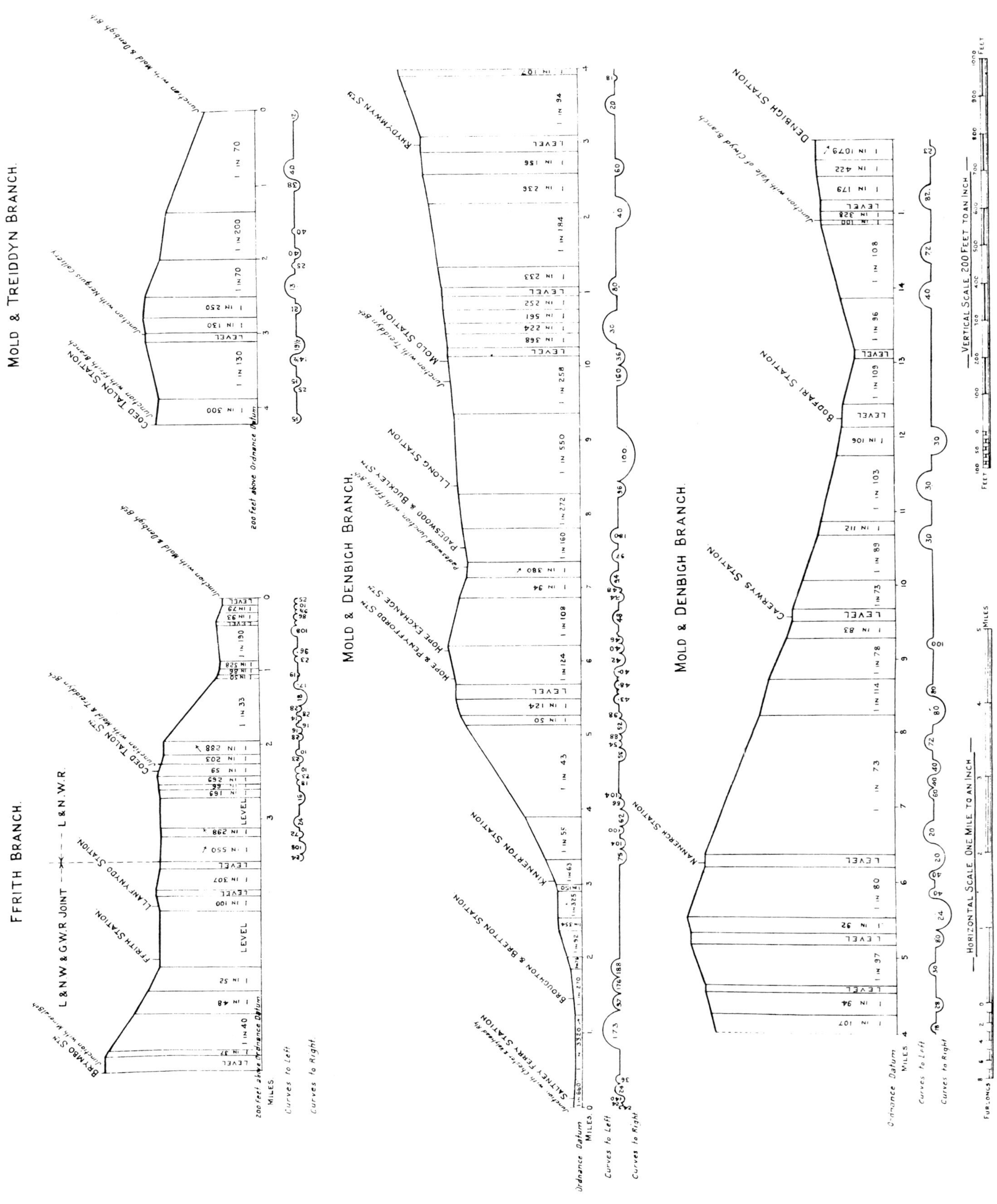
Mold & Treiddyn Branch.
Ffrith Branch.
L & N W. & G.W.R. Joint
L & N. W. R.
Mold & Denbigh Branch.
Mold & Denbigh Branch.
Vertical Scale 200 Feet to an Inch
Horizontal Scale One Mile to an Inch
Coed Talon Station
Brymbo Stn
Ffrith Station.
Llanfynydd Station.
Saltney Ferry Station.
Broughton & Bretton Station.
Kinnerton Station.
Hope & Penyffordd Stn
Hope Exchange Stn
Padeswood & Buckley Stn
Llong Station.
Mold Station.
Rhydymwyn Stn
Nannerch Station.
Caerwys Station.
Bodfari Station.
Denbigh Station.

58. Denbigh. n.d. For the first mile out of Denbigh, the line was double track and worked under Absolute Block regulations as far as Mold & Denbigh Junction signalbox. Here the double track continued towards Mold and Chester, whilst the line to Trefnant and Rhyl became single. The signalbox was of LNWR design, pattern 'D' and of composite construction. It housed a standard LNWR Tumbler frame at 4½" centre, with 20 levers, 12 working and 1 spare. When the line from Bodfari was singled, the junction was removed, the signalbox demolished and trackwork modified to form two parallel single lines as far as the new Denbigh Station box, which replaced the two existing boxes. *British Railways.*

59. Blue Hand Bridge. 4th July 1960. Chester based 2-6-4T No. **42660**, working the 11.41am Ruthin to Chester, passes an Engineer's Special, hauled by one of Rhyl shed's L&Y 0-6-0's, occupying the Down line whilst temporary single line working on the Up line is in operation. This was the preparatory work prior to creating a permanent single line between Bodfari and Denbigh that came into effect the following year. The location is almost identical to the previous picture. Notice the difference in the line side fence on the Up side, and the growth in the vegetation in the intervening years. *D.S. Foulkes Roberts.*

60. Blue Hand Bridge. 1919. This was the first of the summits after leaving Mold & Denbigh Junction signal box, about half way between the junction and Bodfari. The climb on either side was quite steep, but Chester bound traincrews had some respite as they could coast and build up the fire before resuming the climb towards Caerwys. Here, an LNWR 2-4-2T breasts the summit with a Chester train. *D.S. Foulkes Roberts.*

61. Blue Hand Bridge. 13th October 1961. Blue Hand bridge carried the Mold to Rhyl road over the track, and in the early years had proved troublesome. It was subsequently demolished and rebuilt. Local limestone was used in its construction, and the rainfall ensured that it was regularly washed down, always presenting this apparently 'new' look. It provided a spectacular vantage point for viewing the line and photographing trains, particularly looking down the valley towards Bodfari village. *D.S. Foulkes Roberts.*

62. Blue Hand Bridge. 8th September 1961. BR Standard Class 4 4-6-0 No.**75054**, attached to Mold Junction shed (6B) and working the 12.25pm from Ruthin to Chester train, coasts over the summit with three non corridor coaches, safety valves lifting, as it heads for Bodfari. Compare this picture with the two previous views. The former Down line has been lifted, although the single line has not been slued over to the centre of the formation. This was the final season for passenger traffic on the line, but despite this, passenger receipts were very good, and the train was usually well patronised. *D.S. Foulkes Roberts.*

63. Blue Hand bridge. 1919. The LNWR 2-4-2T engines were regular performers on the Chester service from Denbigh, and there was a large contingent of the class based at the shed during this period. They had to work hard and despite the lightweight six coach train, obstacles like the one mile climb at 1 in 108, with the train exposed to the elements on the embankment for most of the way, ensured that the train crew earned their keep. The tank engines were uncomfortable things to work, and were not designed for the comfort of the men. However, judging by the way the safety valves are lifting, there was no shortage of steam in this instance. *D.S. Foulkes Roberts.*

64. Blue Hand Bridge. May 1961. The panoramic view from Blue Hand bridge was one of unspoiled beauty, the track extending away into the distance, crossing Afon Clwyd a few hundred yards from the train. Bodfari village church tower catches the afternoon sun, whilst in the background, mountains of the Clwydian Range dominate the landscape. A Class 2 2-6-0 of the 78xxx class climbs the bank with its two coach train, approaching the bridge which marked the summit of this section of the line before commencing the final descent into Denbigh. *Norman Jones.*

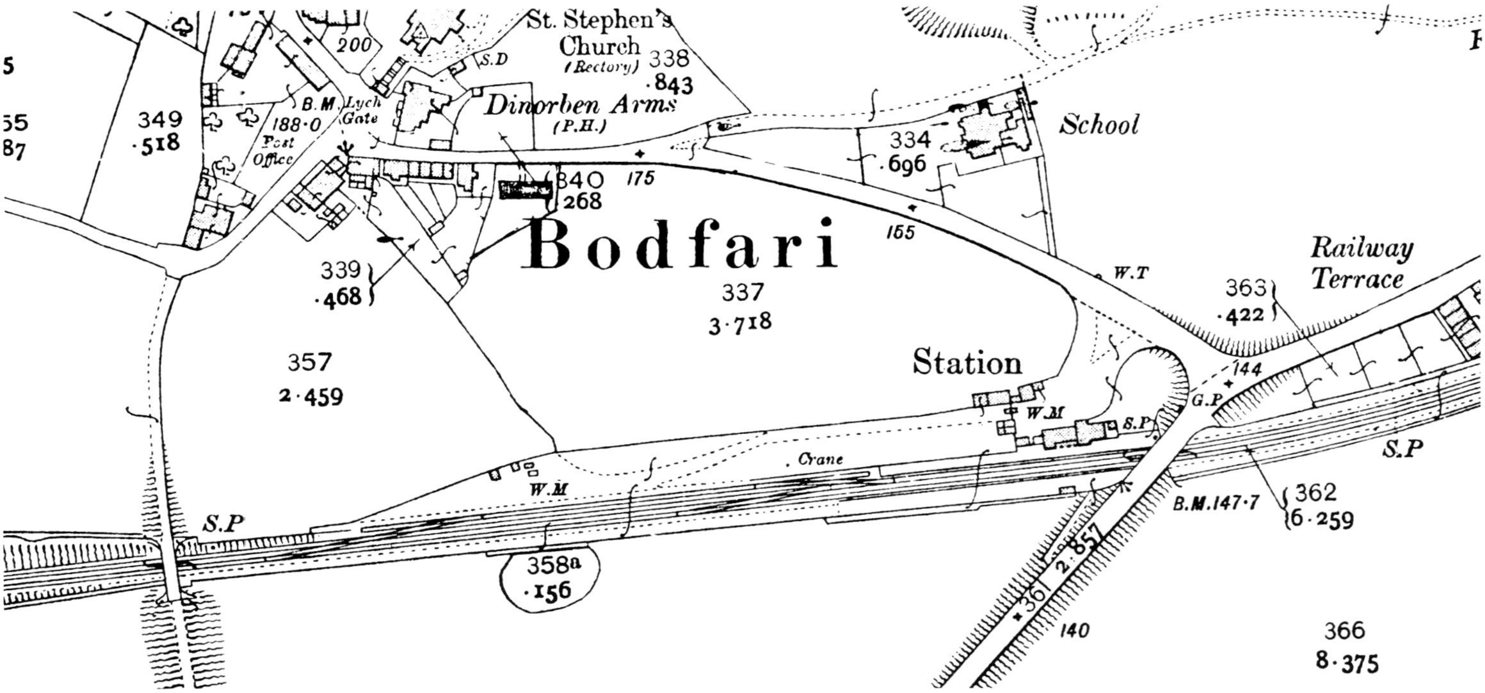
St. Stephen's
Church
(Rectory)
Dinorben Arms
(P.H.)
School
Bodfari
Railway
Terrace
Station
B.M. 188·0
Lych Gate
Post Office
W.T
W.M
S.P
G.P
Crane
B.M.147·7
349
·518
339
·468
357
2·459
337
3·718
338
·843
340
·268
334
·696
363
·422
362
6·259
358a
·156
361
2·857
366
8·375

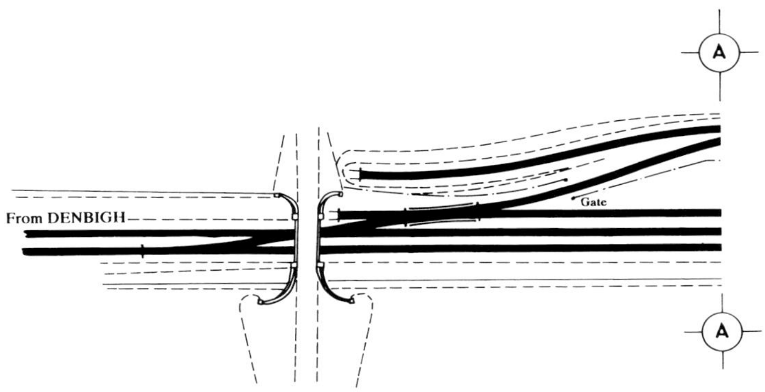
From DENBIGH
Gate
A

BODFARI

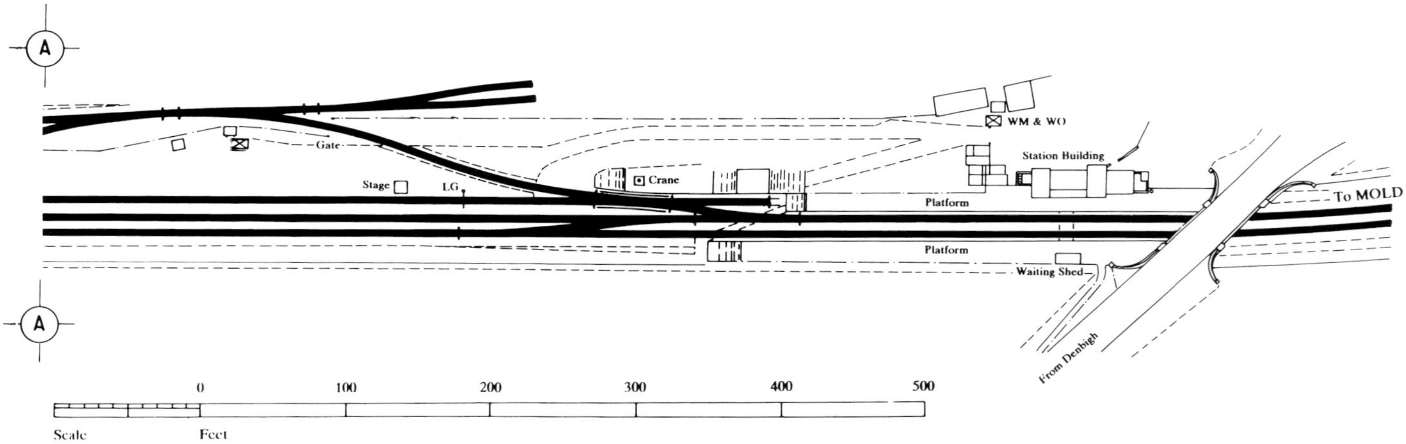
A
Gate
WM & WO
Station Building
Stage
LG
Crane
Platform
Platform
Waiting Shed
To MOLD
From Denbigh
0
100
200
300
400
500
Scale
Feet

65. Bodfari. 22nd May 1955. The station buildings on the Mold & Denbigh Junction line were generally similar in appearance. This one survived the closure of the line and is now a private residence. The small shed adjoining the main building on the Up platform was the goods store, and as traffic declined, fell into disuse. Most small consignments were stored in the station office. Beyond the station is the overbridge that carried the Mold to Denbigh road across the line. The gradient alters at the Chester end of the platform, and the line climbs steadily for the next few miles, stiffening from 1 in 106 at the station, to 1 in 73 approaching Caerwys. *W.A. Camwell.*

Bodfari

Bodfari station opened to traffic from 12th September 1869. Located 3 miles 1154 yards from Denbigh, the line was on the level at the station. From the junction at Mold & Denbigh Junction, the line had fallen on a gradient of 1 in 108 for about a mile, stiffening to 1 in 96 for a further three quarters of a mile before levelling out prior to climbing to Bodfari station at 1 in 109. The track was perfectly straight for nearly two miles, and one could see Up trains approaching under Blue Hand bridge, where the road to St.Asaph passed over the line. Until 1957, the section to Mold & Denbigh Junction signalbox was double track, but from Sunday 5th May the Down line was taken out of service, and lifted. Webb & Thompson train key token equipment, square in shape, coloured blue and lettered Denbigh-Bodfari, was installed, and the section extended to the new Denbigh Station box. New Up distant and home signals replaced the original ones and similarly new Down home and starting signals were installed. The Down starter was located in the path of the former Down line. Track circuiting was installed and the single line token equipment located in the station office.

The main buildings, which included the Station Master's house ,were located on the Up platform, together with a wooden store. A small goods yard lay at the Denbigh end on the Up side, with two sidings. Facilities included a weigh bridge and office, a coal merchant's office and a small yard crane. A private siding left the goods yard through gates to a quarry owned by the Partington Iron & Steel Co. Ltd. Provision was made for wagon storage and run round facilities on privately owned land. The line from the quarry was double, to a point where it connected with the private run round loop. The double track private line crossed a minor road on the level. From 1st January 1951, the agreement between the Partington Steel & Iron Co. Ltd. dated 14th August 1923, was taken over by Mr A. D. H. Pennant. It is not known what traffic emanated from the quarry nor is it known when the rail connection was taken out.

The Down platform had a rudimentary wooden shelter but little else for protection. Passengers had to book their tickets in the office and then cross to the Down platform using the road bridge and a long ramp. An LNW 5 ins. centres, type K.1. frame, with a set of eight levers, which originally controlled 3 points and 6 signals, was located on the Up platform between the station building and the road overbridge. When the line was singled, some modifications were made. The station lay on the edge of the village, but there was some commuter traffic to Mold and Denbigh until the last years of service. After closure, the station yard continued to be used by the local coal merchant. The station buildings were converted into private accommodation. The road bridge was eventually removed and the level of the road dropped as part of a re-alignmeny project.

66. Bodfari. 28th August 1961. Taken from the window of a Chester bound train, we see that the Up Home signal, complete with sight-screen and track-circuit diamond on the post and standing in the Down line formation since the line was singled from here to Denbigh, is 'off' for admission to the Up platform.
D.S. Foulkes Roberts.

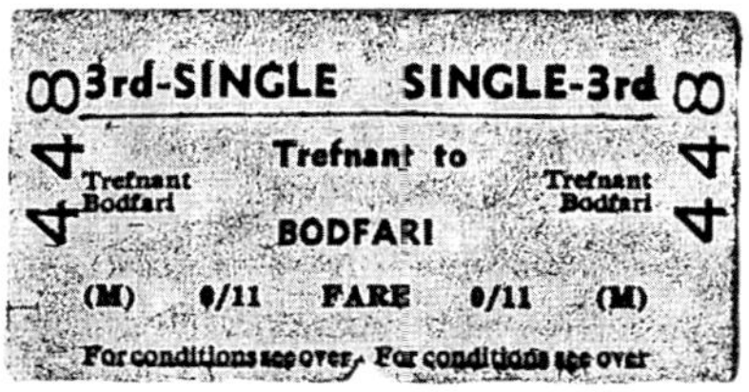

67. Bodfari. 18th September 1961. By that date this photograph was taken, Bodfari goods yard had lost most of its freight traffic, with only the local coal merchant still receiving deliveries by rail. At one time a private siding led off the yard to local quarries, where limestone was loaded and worked away to steel and ironworks, but this traffic had ceased by 1952. The remnants of a yard crane stand on the loading wharf, a solitary loading gauge stands guard over No.1. siding which housed a single wagon. In the distance, the weigh bridge office stands deserted. Notice the complex pointwork in the yard, which survived until the track was lifted. *D.S. Foulkes Roberts.*

68. Bodfari. 1919. This view shows details of the platform side of the main building, with clear signs indicating the Booking Office, Ladies Waiting Room, etc. Two members of staff watch the Chester bound train draw to a halt. In the background can be seen carts in the goods yard and above this the fencing can be identified that marked the boundary between the LNWR's land and the private siding that led to the Limestone Quarry.
D.S. Foulkes Roberts.

69. Bodfari. 18th September 1961. Another look at the Up side platform and buildings, taken from the window of a Chester train. The guard looks back to ensure his train has not divided, still clutching the green flag, whilst a porter signalman stands in front of the station office, ready to move to the lever frame between the building and the bridge abutment, in order to return the Starter signal to danger. The wooden shed was a small goods store, but latterly out of use, the small consignments received could be accommodated in the station office. The station building survived closure, and is now a private dwelling. The road bridge was removed when the level was dropped, in road improvement schemes in the early 1970's. *D.S. Foulkes Roberts.*

70. Bodfari. September 1959. On the Up platform, between the station buildings and the abutments of the bridge that carried the Mold to Denbigh road over the line, this eight lever standard Webb design LNWR frame controlled traffic movements in the station limits. Lever 8 was spare, and had even lost the stirrup that released the catch. There was minimal protection for the signal indicators, the signal frame diagram appears to have leaked and is water stained. One of the two Annett's keys is visible behind lever 5. Illumination was provided by the oil lamp mounted on its post, which seems somewhat out of true! The single line token instrument for the section of line to Denbigh was located in the station office. *Norman Jones.*

71. Bodfari. September 1959. The main station building incorporated the Station Master's house, and provided a general waiting room and ladies waiting room as well as the usual offices and toilets. Platform furniture was fairly limited, consisting of oil lamps along the platforms and in front of the booking office door, together with a station nameboard and wooden seat under the shade of the small canopy. Denbigh bound passengers were expected to cross the line using the road bridge, which involved a lengthy walk, whilst staff were provided with a boarded walk-way in front of the office. Judging by the worn coping stones, there had been extensive use made of this crossing in the past! The Up Starting signal nestles under the shade of the bridge. Notice the telegraph post and abundance of wires, now rarely seen. On the house chimneys, two old style 405 line television aerials protrude, one aimed at Winter Hill transmitter, whilst the other is directed towards Llanddona on Anglesey, to pick up the Welsh programmes beamed from there. *Norman Jones.*

72.Bodfari. 14th June 1961. The approach to Bodfari station, seen from the coach of a Chester to Ruthin train at the commencement of the sweeping curve. The gradient is steep, and the Up line is protected by a catch-point that would divert the runaway into the field rather than just derailing it into the ballast. The village of Bodfari was clustered around a road junction, and can be seen to the right hand side of the picture. Notice the occupation crossing in the foreground, with the bi-lingual warning signs facing the gate.
D.S. Foulkes Roberts

73. Bodfari. 28th August 1961. The same occupation crossing as seen in the previous picture, this time looking towards Caerwys. In the distance is the Bodfari Down distant signal, and the bi-lingual warning notices facing the path to the crossing. The track was relaid in 1960 with modern concrete sleeper chaired track, and was subsequently recovered for use elsewhere when the line closed. The hillsides closed in on the line as it weaved its way along the valley.
D.S. Foulkes Roberts.

74.Between Bodfari and Caerwys. 28th August 1961. About half way between Bodfari and Caerwys the line passes under a minor road bridge, curving and twisting to follow the valley contours, whilst climbing steadily to the summit beyond Star Crossing. The driver of the 2-6-4T keeps a steady vigil on the track, the safety valves simmering despite the climb. These engines were ideally suited for this kind of work and firemen had little difficulty in keeping up steam pressure.
D.S. Foulkes Roberts.

75. Between Bodfari and Caerwys. April 1961. An unidentified Stanier 2-6-4T hauls two non corridor coaches on a Chester to Ruthin working in the early spring of 1961. At this point the line follows the valley floor, and crosses a small brook, seen here from the Mold to Denbigh road, roughly half way between the two villages. On the hillside, farm houses stand out, freshly white-washed, whilst the trees have not yet produced the new growth, giving everywhere a somewhat bleak look. *Norman Jones.*

76. Between Bodfari and Caerwys. April 1961. The rural nature of the line is captured in this view, as Stanier 2-6-4T with its two non corridor coaches coasts towards Bodfari, safety valves simmering. In the background, the Forestry Commission had prepared the ground for planting, whilst a cottage nestles under the side of the hill. In the foreground, the sheep seem unconcerned as the train passes. Apart from the growth of the vegetation in the forestry plantation and the removal of the track, little has changed in the intervening years. *Norman Jones.*

77. Caerwys. 22nd May 1957. This view shows details of the Up side, taken from the Down platform. The main station buildings are similar in design to those at Bodfari, Nannerch and Rhydymwyn and included the Station Master's residence as well as the usual offices. Behind the platform can be seen the timber yard that generated much traffic. Beyond the station is the single road goods shed. Passengers crossed from the Up to the Down line over the track at the Mold end of the platform, whilst staff used the walk-way outside the station office. Crosville buses from Holywell via Caerwys village used to terminate outside the station and for many years after the war, Bristol type 'L' single decker vehicles based at Flint worked this service. One is seen here outside the main station entrance. *W.A. Camwell.*

Caerwys

Caerwys station was 2 miles 1007 yards from Bodfari, and probably the busiest intermediate station between Mold and Denbigh. The station was actually located at Afonwen, but named to avoid confusion with the station of the same name on the Cambrian coast, and more likely to identify the station with the better known historical township, located on the hillside some distance away from the line. The station limits were on the level, although situated on a rising gradient, mostly at 1 in 73, from milepost 13 to the summit of the line at milepost 5 .

The station consisted of platforms on the Up and Down lines with the main buildings and station forecourt on the Up side. The Down platform had the usual basic shelter,a "design" adopted for numerous locations on the line. Passengers crossed the line on a barrow crossing at the ramps at the Mold end. The buildings on both platforms were similar in appearance and layout to those at Bodfari.

There was an eight lever open frame on the platform of type K.1. According to the LNWR 1910 list of signalboxes and frames, this controlled 4 points and 8 signals. There was a siding behind the platform on the Up side, with a connection off the Down line to the Dock Siding frame, and which was controlled by an Annetts Key A from the station frame. This siding was used for loading timber, the local sawmill operating within the yard, and which still exists today. Another Down siding was at the Mold end of the platform, operated by the Down Siding frame and similarly controlled by Annetts Key A from the station frame. At one time this extended to an Iron Foundry. The main goods yard was on the Up side at the Mold end and controlled from the Yard frame which itself was controlled by Annetts Key B from the station frame. The trailing connection led to a single road through the goods shed before terminating in stops by the platform ramp. A second siding was used for coal traffic with a third line leading to two private sidings, one of which was alongside a cement shed and which were owned by the British Portland Cement Manufacturers Ltd. On the main line, a trailing crossover was located level with the goods shed.

Crosville Motor Services Ltd. commenced a bus service in 1923 from Holywell to Caerwys station through Caerwys village, and buses met most trains. This was CMS route 45, and operated by single deck vehicles. The service survived and buses continued to terminate in the station yard for several years after the line closed until the mid 1970's when the route proved uneconomic to maintain and the service ceased.

78. Caerwys. 5th May 1961. The length of the platforms at Caerwys somehow seemed generous, considering the usual train formation that used the line, when two or three coach trains were the norm, emphasised by this view taken from the ramp at the Denbigh end looking towards Mold. This station was responsible for handling a lot of the freight traffic that passed over the line, particularly timber, and the proprietors of the concern had a large yard adjoining the station, and which still survives to this day, as do the station buildings. Beyond the station can be seen a factory chimney. At one time an Iron Works was established there, and also provided traffic to and from the foundry. *D. Thompson.*

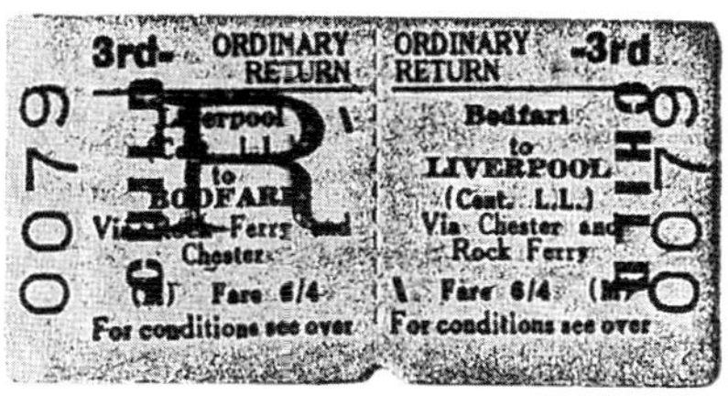

CAERWYS

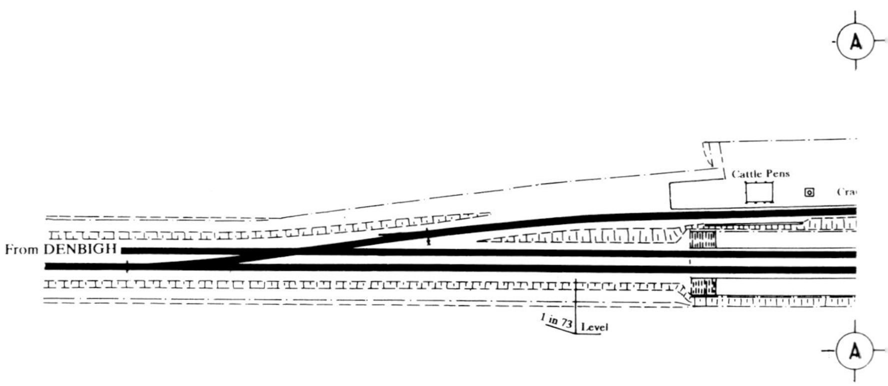

79. Caerwys. c.1960. Caerwys station, taken from the six foot at the Denbigh end of station and looking towards Mold. Just visible in the long grass is a short siding, used for loading timber, with a yard crane alongside. The Down line has been relaid with concrete sleepers through the station, as the new ballast indicates. On the Down side, the Foundry chimney towers over the main factory building. The line continues climbing beyond the station and the change in gradient is obvious. A Denbigh train is signalled but not yet visible. There is little sign of passengers or staff. *I. Vaughan*

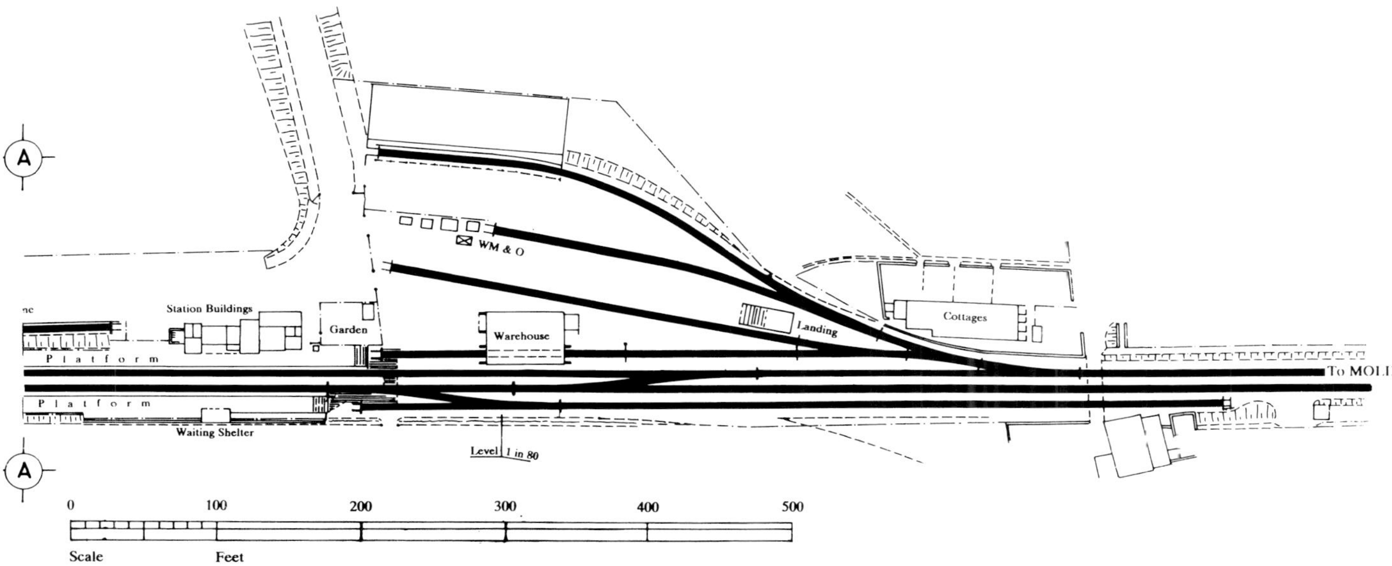

80. Caerwys. 17th April 1962. A BR Standard Class 4 4-6-0 pulls away from Caerwys station on a return working to Chester. The driver acknowledges the guard's signal whilst a member of the station staff keeps a watchful eye on the photographer. The goods shed is obliterated by escaping steam from the locomotive's drain cocks, whilst the black smoke indicates that the fireman is attending to his duties. These Chester based carriage workings must have been some of the few remaining in North Wales to regularly use non corridor stock. *D.S. Foulkes Roberts.*

81. Caerwys. 17th April 1962. The photographer and his brother travelled to Caerwys in the penultimate week of service. Here the guard loads a bicycle into the guards van whilst a porter climbs from the track and onto the platform behind the train with a parcel. Note the open front shelter. On a wet day, such as this one, it provided little shelter against the elements and certainly no comfort. *D.S. Foulkes Roberts.*

82.(left) **Caerwys. n.d.** The goods warehouse was an imposing structure, but it must have justified its construction. It consisted of a single road, with vehicular access and a loading platform inside, complete with a small hand crane. The warehouse line passed through the shed and terminated in rail built stops at the foot of the Up platform ramp. Immediately alongside the stops was the Up starter, a standard LNWR square shaped wooden post lower quadrant fixture, with the ladder passing in front of the signal arm. Beyond the warehouse can be seen the chimney and building of the former foundry. *I. Vaughan.*

83. Caerwys. 1961. Apart from trials to determine the suitability of using Diesel Multiple Units along the branch in 1956, when empty workings were conducted for a week or so, they were never used on ordinary service trains. However, the RCTS organised a trip over the line and this view, taken from the leading cab, shows the approach to Caerwys station on the Down side. The siding on the left was formerly connected with the foundry, although little used latterly. On the Up side, the goods shed and office are clearly seen, together with the occupation crossing immediately in front of the cab. *G.H. Platt.*

84. Caerwys. c.1960. In common with several other stations on the line, no signal boxes were provided, merely a lever frame mounted on the platform and exposed to the elements. At Caerwys it was located on the Mold side of the main buildings, on the Up platform, and consisted of a standard LNW Webb design eight lever frame, type K1, of which lever 5 was spare, although in this case, not painted white as was the practice. These controlled signals. Three Annett's keys on the frame were provided: Key 'A' controlled the Down Siding Frame, Key 'B' controlled the Yard Frame, whilst Key 'C' controlled the crossover frame and the Dock Siding Frame. The indicators were protected by rudimentary covers. *I. Vaughan.*

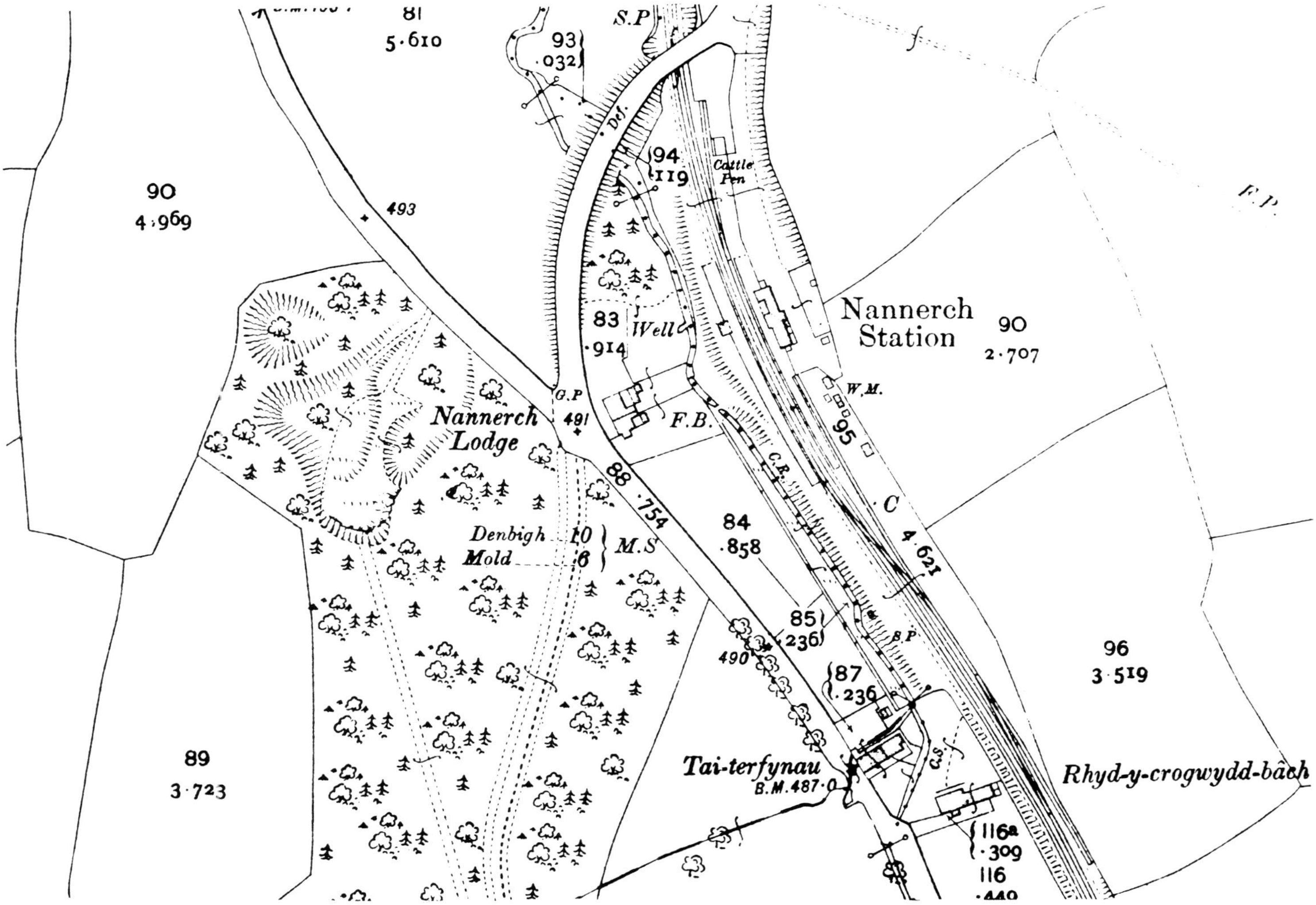

85. Nannerch. 5th May 1961. This view, in the author's opinion, epitomises the LMS country station. The Up platform buildings are uniform with other stations on the Mold & Denbigh section of line. The station approach is between an avenue of mature trees and there is an almost timeless air about this scene. Alas, although the station was purchased privately, it was subsequently demolished in a road improvement scheme. *D. Thompson.*

86. Nannerch. 22nd April 1957. Another view of the station buildings on the Up platform, this time looking towards Denbigh. At one time the cement rendering had been painted, but when this photograph was taken, had faded and peeled, presenting an untidy appearance. There is some apparent clutter around the shed, but generally the station was kept tidy. Alongside the enclosed house yard is a standard open platform mounted 8-lever frame of LNW pattern, for controlling signals. Lever No.5 was spare. Points were controlled by two-lever ground frames alongside the track. *W.A. Camwell.*

Nannerch

3 miles 648 yards from Caerwys, the line ran under the main Mold to Denbigh road and into Nannerch station. The station was about half a mile from Nannerch village and as before, the rising gradient levelled out from its 1 in 73 climb before resuming at 1 in 80 to the summit of the line which was reached just under a mile further on towards Mold, shortly before Star Crossing halt. The station was on a long left-handed sweeping curve with reverse curves of varying radii on the rail approach on either side of the station. A private road approached the station was from the Mold to Denbigh road, just before the bridge over the line, and passed between an avenue of mature trees, creating an idyllic setting which, in the author's opinion, was one which epitomised the rural branch line station.

The station building was of the same uniform design as Bodfari and Caerwys, with cement rendered walls, and similarly located on the Up platform, with the Station Master's house part of the building. Passengers crossed the line at the Denbigh end of the platform, down the ramp and across the barrow crossing. The Down platform had a very simple basic shelter, open to the tracks, and devoid of comfort.

At the Caerwys end, a short trailing siding from the Up line led to a cattle dock, controlled by a small two lever frame. An LNW type K.I. eight lever open frame stood on the Up platform controlling four points and seven signals, with lever No.5 spare.

A small goods yard was located at the Mold end of the station on the Up side, with access from the Up line by a trailing point. Connection was made from the siding to the Down line. There was limited wagon capacity. A small wooden shed in the yard served as a goods store. Incoming freight traffic to the station was slight, probably coal and animal feedstuff, with some livestock traffic working out from time to time.

In the last year of traffic, the daily morning freight service from Denbigh to Mold Junction was withdrawn and replaced by a daily freight train from Denbigh to Nannerch, (Saturdays Excepted) which shunted at Bodfari and Caerwys on the outward journey. It arrived there at 11.36am and had half an hour to shunt before working back to Denbigh.

The station building and goods yard was purchased shortly after closure. The building was completely renovated, the platforms removed and the whole area landscaped. Unfortunately the work was in vain, for within months of completion, the site was purchased under compulsory order, and demolished to make way for road improvements which removed the bridge over the trackbed.

87. Nannerch. 14th June 1961. Chester trains ran into Nannerch station under the Mold to Denbigh road bridge, the Up Home signal post giving good visibility to train crews above the road level. A short trailing siding, controlled by an Annett's key, led to a cattle loading dock. The barrow crossing at the foot of the ramp was also used by passengers to cross the line to the Down platform. At night, an oil lamp in a standard container gave some illumination. A standard enamel station nameboard was provided, and apart from other oil lamps, was the extent of the platform furniture. The flower beds adjoining the platform are but a shadow of their former beauty. Presumably the staff who tended them in their less busy moments have moved away, or lost interest, as proposed closure notices had been posted by this date. *D.S. Foulkes Roberts.*

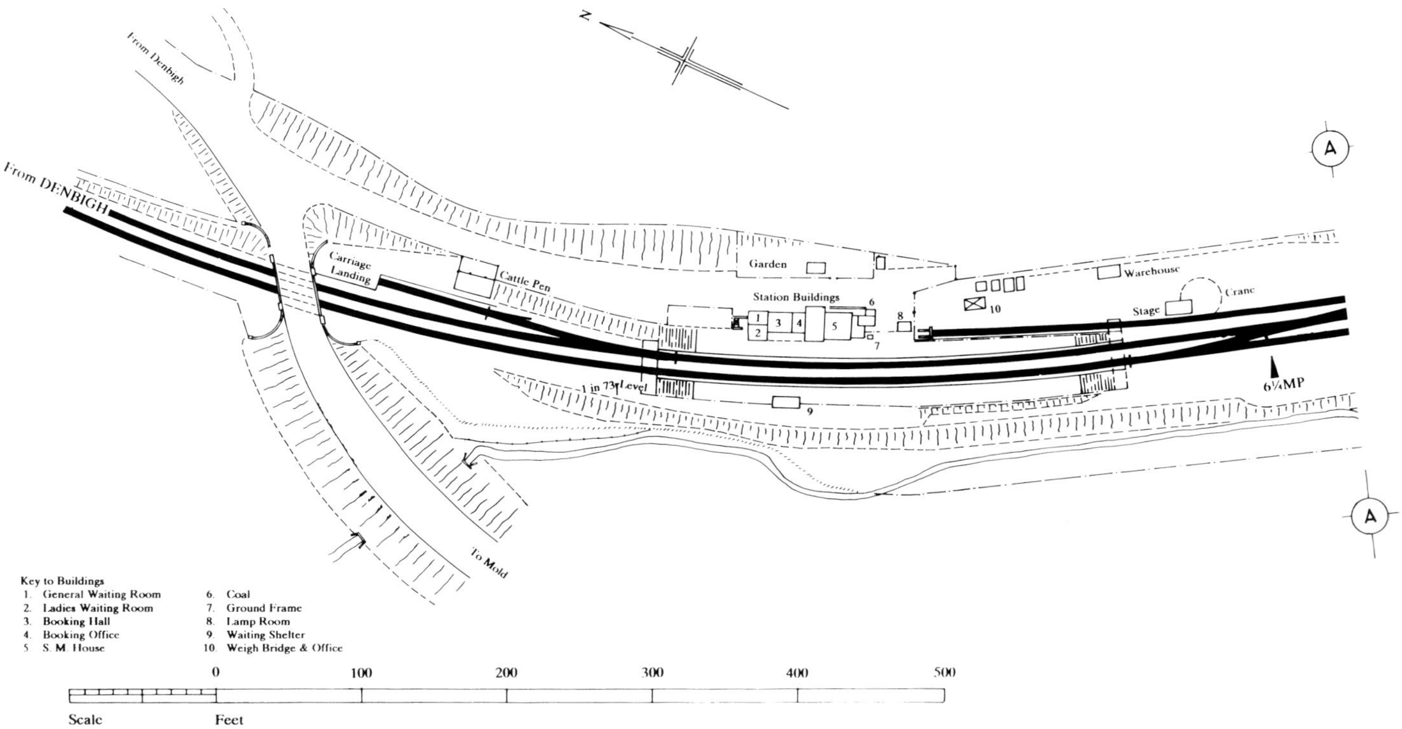

88. Nannerch. 23rd April 1959. A solitary passenger from a Denbigh bound train walks along the Up platform, heading for the booking hall and the exit. Frequently there were no passengers, as the station was about half a mile from the village, and buses from Mold terminated in the centre of the village. The station was well looked after by its staff, who had plenty of time between trains to keep everything tidy, and until closure was threatened, kept attractive flower beds and shrubs with ornaments as part of their routine tasks. *R.J. Buckley.*

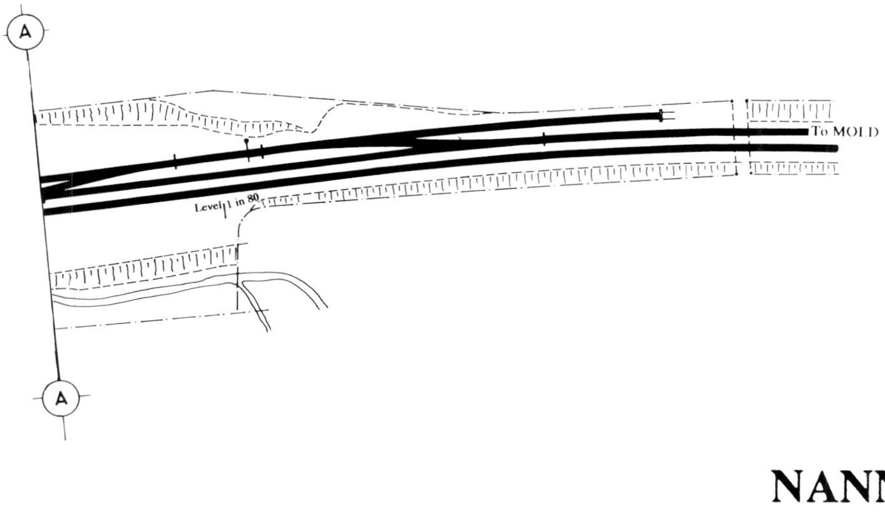

NANNERCH

89. Nannerch. n.d. Another view of the station buildings on the Up platform, the similarities between it and others on the line can be noted. The Down platform was more basic. An open fronted waiting shed and a few oil lamps sufficed. A small yard on the Up side, which contained a coal siding, sufficed with access from the Up and Down lines. A small shed in the yard was used as a store. Inward freight traffic was usually confined to coal for the local merchant, although some livestock was transported from time to time. *I. Vaughan.*

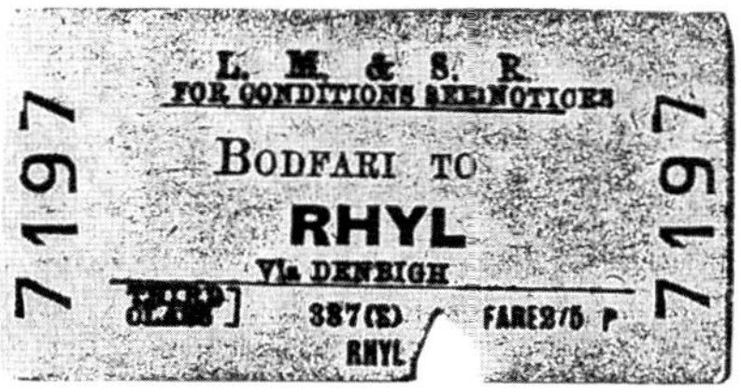

90. Nannerch. 28th August 1961. Memories of a bygone age! There is a haunting atmosphere about this view, three passengers walking up the platform towards the guard, who has opened a carriage door in readiness for them. The station buildings are featureless, and there is the minimum of furniture. An oil lamp in its wall mounted case, a sack truck just visible by the corner of the building. The platforms, equally bare, but clean. Beyond the Up starter, the track curves away towards Star Crossing. Alas, all swept away, replaced by the ribbon of tarmac that passes for progress. *D.S. Foulkes Roberts.*

91. Nannerch. n.d. The Mold end of Nannerch station, showing the goods yard, with one wagon in the siding. A small shed in the yard served as a store. Modern upper quadrant signals serve as Up Starter and Down Home, the former on a tubular post. The goods yard and crossover points are controlled by two-lever ground frames. In the goods loop a loading gauge straddles the track. A close-up view of a Down platform oil lamp dominates this view. *I. Vaughan.*

92. Star Crossing Halt. 5th May 1961. The Up and Down platforms at Star Crossing, looking towards Mold and Chester, and taken from the level crossing. Notice the absence of shelter on the Down side. Presumably, passengers waited in the Crossing Keeper's cottage until the train was imminent and then made their way to the platform. The Up platform fared better, having a semi enclosed shed for shelter. Apart from two oil lamps in glass cases on each platform, each with paper name stickers to inform, there was no other method of identifying the location. *D. Thompson.*

Star Crossing

Located 73 chains from Nannerch and 18 miles 55 chains from Chester, on the Denbigh side of the summit of the line, Star Crossing consisted of two platforms about 150ft long. The halt was opened on 2nd November 1914 and closed temporarily from 1st January 1917 until 1st July 1919. Apart from a couple of cottages and the Crossing Keeper's house by the station, there were no other dwellings close by, the village of Cilcain being the closest settlement, nearly two miles away, the road from which connected with the Mold to Denbigh road at Star Crossing.

The Down platform was devoid of shelter, presumably any passengers waited in the Crossing Keeper's house, which also served as a booking office. A couple of oil lamps, mounted on wooden posts, and a post mounted information board doubled as a name board, which completed the furniture. Access to the platform from the cottage was by a short footpath alongside the line, bounded by fencing. The Up platform boasted a small wooden hut giving rudimentary shelter. Access from the cottage was across the level crossing, the gates of which were normally across the tracks and open to road users, and through a gate to an enclosed footpath to the platform. Apart from the shelter, two oil lamps mounted on posts completed the inventory. The station name was adhered on the lamp housings. The level crossing gates were hand operated, and a small hut 8ft by 8ft housed a two lever frame which controlled signals.

Most trains called at the halt, some by request, and despite the isolated location and lack of passengers, the halt remained open to traffic until the line closed.

93. Star Crossing Halt. 14th June 1961. A BR Standard Class 4 4-6-0 stands on the level crossing at the halt with a three coach Chester to Ruthin working, although it does not appear that anyone is inconvenienced. Passengers booked their tickets in the Crossing Keeper's house, and those bound for Mold and Chester were obliged to walk along a narrow fenced path to gain the platform. Frequently however, they walked alongside the track, taking care not to trespass onto the keeper's allotment. *D.S. Foulkes Roberts.*

94. Star Crossing. n.d. The Down platform at Star Crossing was devoid of shelter, and furniture consisted of two oil lamps and a poster-board. The platform was edged in concrete slabs, infilled with compacted rubble. Booking facilities were provided at the crossing keeper's house that stood at the foot of the ramp behind the photographer. A solitary passenger walks towards the exit, whilst the crossing keeper stands to relay the guard's signal to the traincrew.
Author's collection.

95. Star Crossing Halt. 23rd April 1959. Another view of the Up platform and shelter at Star Crossing, taken from a Down train. The solitary lamp on the platform was supplemented by another inside the shelter, and which possibly gave some heat to comfort the waiting traveller. About a hundred yards towards Mold the gradient changed from rising to falling. This was the summit of the line, where traincrews had some respite and where they could relax if they had been short of steam, and put on the injector to fill up the boiler and allow pressure to rise. *R.J. Buckley.*

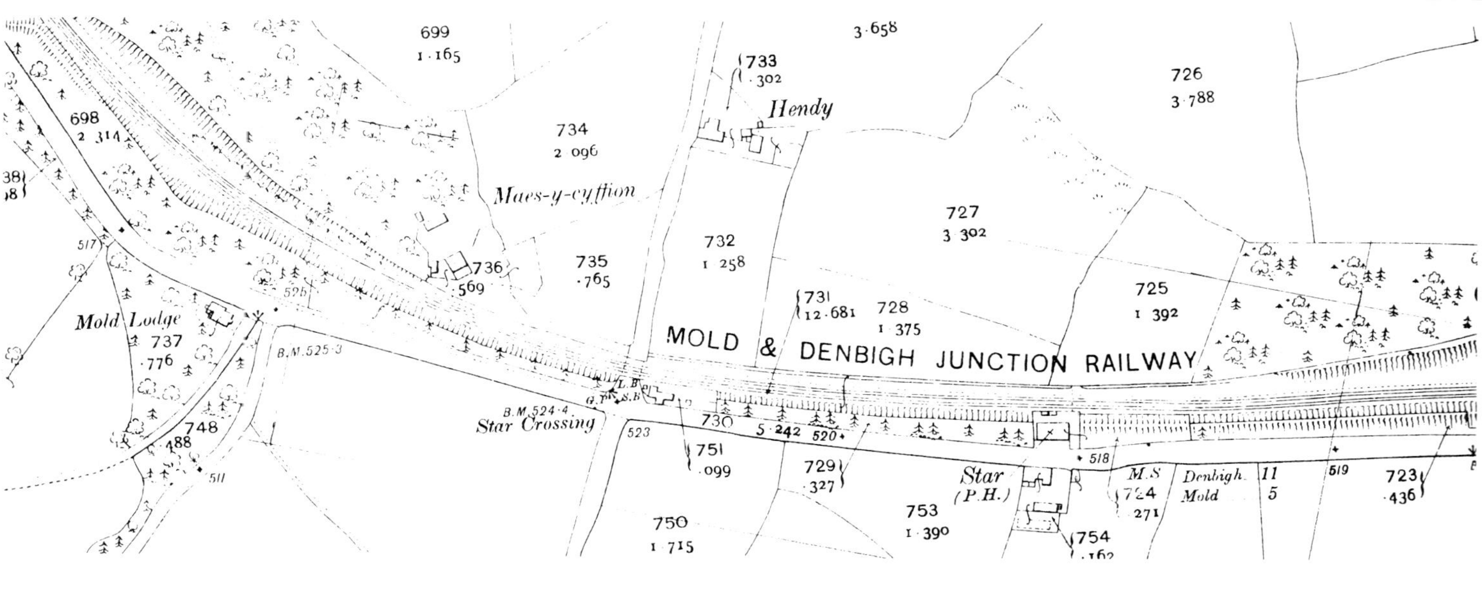

96. Star Crossing Halt. 18th September 1961. Some extent of the limited space available on the Up platform is gained by this view, showing a three coach Chester bound train receiving the guard's flag, whilst he keeps a watchful eye on the couple who are intending to trespass and cross the line at the foot of the ramp and not over the appointed place. The locomotive and the third coach are both off the platform, and it would have been necessary to draw up twice had anyone got into the last coach by mistake. Guards however, knew everyone on the line, and ensured that this was prevented.

D.S. Foulkes Roberts.

97. Star Crossing Halt. 18th August 61. The approach to Star Crossing, taken from a Chester to Denbigh train, showing the short Down side platform, with the Crossing Keeper's cottage and the level crossing beyond. The train has just passed the summit of the line, and apart for the mile beyond Bodfari, is mainly down hill all the way to Denbigh. Beyond the halt, the line is briefly hemmed in by the surrounding hillside but widens out again after a few hundred yards.

D.S. Foulkes Roberts.

Hendre Siding

Located 1 mile 15 chains from Star Crossing Halt, Hendre Siding signal box consisted of a standard LNWR Type 'D' cabin of composite construction, and a set of 20 levers of which six were spare. The line at this point was on an embankment in the narrowest part of the valley, with the road, railway and stream hemmed in by rocky outcrop on either side. The line crossed the main Mold to Denbigh road twice in a short distance. The signal cabin was on the Up side, and controlled a trailing crossover on the main line, to a loop and sidings on the Down side, which served limestone quarries. A short distance towards Rhydymwyn was the siding to the Hendre Lime Works which made a trailing connection to the Up line, and similarly controlled from the signal box. Latterly the box was only manned on Mondays to Saturdays between 1.25pm and 1.45pm, and a porter signalman from Rhydymwyn switched the box into the circuit.

98 (above). **Hendre Sidings. 28th August 1961.** Between Star Crossing Halt and Rhydymwyn, the line is supervised by two signal boxes which controls access to freight sidings. Travelling towards Chester, the first is at Hendre Siding, a standard LNWR design type 'D' composite box which housed a twenty lever frame, and was located on the Up side. The box remained in use until the line closed to through traffic, although latterly it had diminished in importance. This view shows the box, taken from a Chester bound train. Notice the sighting boards which were necessary at certain time of day when the sun shone into the driver's eyes as the train rounded the corner. The village of Hendre is below the level of the line, and during winter months, never gets any direct sunlight.

D.S. Foulkes Roberts.

99 (centre). **Hendre Sidings. 18th September 1961.** Another view of Hendre Siding signal box, this time taken from a Chester to Denbigh train, and seen here, looking towards Denbigh. At this point the Mold to Denbigh road passes under the line twice within a hundred yards or so, in a horse-shoe shaped curve, The road can be seen in the bottom right hand corner of the picture. Trees mask Hendre Limestone Quarry, which was acquired by Alfred McAlpine & Co. and reopened in 1959 after several years of disuse, to supply limestone for the construction of the Preston By-pass, now part of the M6.

D.S. Foulkes Roberts.

100 (left). **Hendre Sidings. 14th June 1961.** Freight traffic, mainly limestone, was worked away from Hendre Siding until shortly before the line closed, and access to the sidings

(continued on page 71)

100 (*continued*)
was controlled from Hendre Siding signal box. These were located on the Down side of the line, and before the war it was the practice at times to 'trip' some workings from Mold according to demand. Otherwise, Denbigh to Mold Junction Class 'K' freight trains called and picked up loaded wagons. Empty mineral wagons were dropped off by Mold to Denbigh trains, which left the brake van on the main line before setting back into the siding where the wagons would be uncoupled and disposed of by the quarry staff.
D.S. Foulkes Roberts.

101 (right-top). **Hendre Sidings. 18th September 1961.** Halkyn Lime Works siding was also controlled by Hendre Sidings box, and located on the Up side between Hendre and Dolfechlas. As can be seen from this view, there was substantial traffic from the works, with four wagons and one van in the siding, and it was usual to uplift four or five vehicles each day. Fine ground lime was bagged and loaded into vans, the remainder carried in open or hopper wagons, some of which was for railway use.
D.S. Foulkes Roberts.

102 (centre). **Hendre Sidings. 28th August 1961.** A Chester to Ruthin train passes over the Mold to Denbigh road bridge, hauled by one of Mold Junction's BR Standard Class 4 4-6-0's. The signal box is partly obscured by the locomotive smokebox. On the right hand side, partly concealed by the shrubbery, is the quarry and working rock-face of the Halkyn Lime Works. *D.S. Foulkes Roberts.*

103. Hendre Sidings. 14th June 1961. Halkyn Lime Works siding was on the Up side of the line, controlled from Hendre Sidings signal box. Locomotives were not permitted to pass through the gate and it was necessary for the Lime Works to collect the empty and deliver the loaded wagons and vans to the gate. Notice the catch point in the siding, secured by a single lever and locked by an Annett's key supplied by the signalman on duty.
D.S. Foulkes Roberts.

Dolfechlas Crossing

Like Hendre Siding, there was no passenger provision here, the signal box controlling a road level crossing and access to the Ruby Brick & Tile Company and the Olwyn Goch Lead Mine sidings. The signal box was standard LNWR type 'E', of composite construction, which housed a set of 22 levers. In 1910, this controlled 6 points and 10 signals. At the time of lifting the line, the box had five working, and seventeen spare levers. The level crossing gates were hand operated. It was located 1156 yards from Hendre Siding, and 1149 yards from Rhydymwyn, on the Up side. Apart from controlling access to the siding, facing and trailing crossovers were located on either side of the level crossing. When passenger traffic ceased in 1962 there was still a reasonable quantity of freight despatched from the brick works which ensured the line's retention. The Up line was lifted back to Rhydymwyn, with the Down line left in place as far as the crossing, where it briefly crossed over to the Up side via the facing crossover to connect with the siding. It then reverted to the Down side using the trailing crossover, and extended a short distance, sufficient to hold 35 wagons and a brake, before terminating in a new stop block. Both Up and Down lines to Denbigh were lifted from these points. Empty wagon traffic to the Brick Works was propelled from Rhydymwyn.

104 (above). **Dolfechlas Crossing. 28th August 1961.** A Chester bound passenger train from Ruthin passes Hendre Siding Down Distant signal as it approaches Dolfechlas Up Home signal. Alongside the signal can be seen the gated approach to the Ruby Brick Works siding. The Crossing signal box is out of sight round the curve.
D.S. Foulkes Roberts.

105.(centre-left) **Dolfechlas Crossing. 28th August 1961.** Between Nannerch and Rhydymwyn, the line twisted and turned in the valley to avoid excessive changes of gradient. At Dolfechlas Crossing, the valley floor widens out, enabling the curviture of the line to ease somewhat. Here an afternoon working from Denbigh to Chester, hauled by a Stanier 2-6-4T, at the head of three non-corridor coaches, approaches Dolfechlas Crossing Box, which controlled access to the sidings for Olwyn Goch lead mine and the Ruby Brick Works, and which provided regular traffic for the line.
D.S. Foulkes Roberts.

106. Dolfechlas Crossing. April 1962. This was a standard LNW design box, size 'E', of composite construction, and which housed a 22 lever frame. Latterly, 17 levers were spare. and its prime function was to control the level crossing gates to the Ruby Brick Works and the Olwyn Goch Lead Mines. After the line closed to passenger services, a single line remained in use to the Ruby Brick Works. Part of the Down line was retained beyond the level crossing for use as a siding, and was of sufficient length to hold 35 wagons and a brake. The box was demoted to an unmanned ground frame and the gates were padlocked. There was no run round facilities so traffic for the siding was propelled from Rhydymwyn. Notice the lower windows and cabin door window have been boarded over. *I. Vaughan.*

107.Rhydymwyn.14th.June 1961. The guard gives the 'Right Away' to the traincrew of the 1.35pm Chester to Denbigh train, as a porter makes his way to return the signals to danger once the train has departed. The station building was uniform in design with other Mold & Denbigh Junction stations on the line, and survives to this day. The station was conveniently located for the village, and provided much of the passenger traffic to Chester, and which was considerably quicker than the buses which replaced the rail service. *D.S. Foulkes Roberts.*

Rhydymwyn

1149 yards from Dolfechlas Crossing and 13 miles from Mold Junction, the station served the small village of the same name, grouped around the 'Antelope' hotel. The line crossed the Mold to Denbigh road on the level, the gates being hand-operated and locked from the two lever ground frame mounted on the Down platform, usually operated by a porter under the supervision of the Station Master. The main buildings were also on the Down platform and incorporated the Station master's house. The Up platform consisted of the almost standard design rudimentary shelter. Passengers crossed the line at the level crossing. There were goods facilities on both sides of the line, although the goods yard was on the Up side, access to the yard controlled from Rhydymwyn signal cabin, located at the Mold end on the Up side. This consisted of a standard LMS cabin which contained a 45 lever frame, of which 36 were working levers. The signal box was manned throughout the working day, latterly from 6.15am until 9.40pm. The War Ministry established a factory on the Down side of the line during World War Two, and additional sidings were installed and connected with the works. This provided a much needed boost to the traffic working over the line, and although the exact nature of what was manufactured during the war period and after was never disclosed, the complex was listed as a site of strategic importance for many years, and security was extremely tight. Latterly Rhydymwyn became the terminus of the line following the cessation of passenger traffic. After the track was uplifted beyond Dolfechlas Crossing, locomotives ran round their stock in the station platform lines, and any traffic for Dolfechlas and Halkyn Lime Works was propelled from the station.

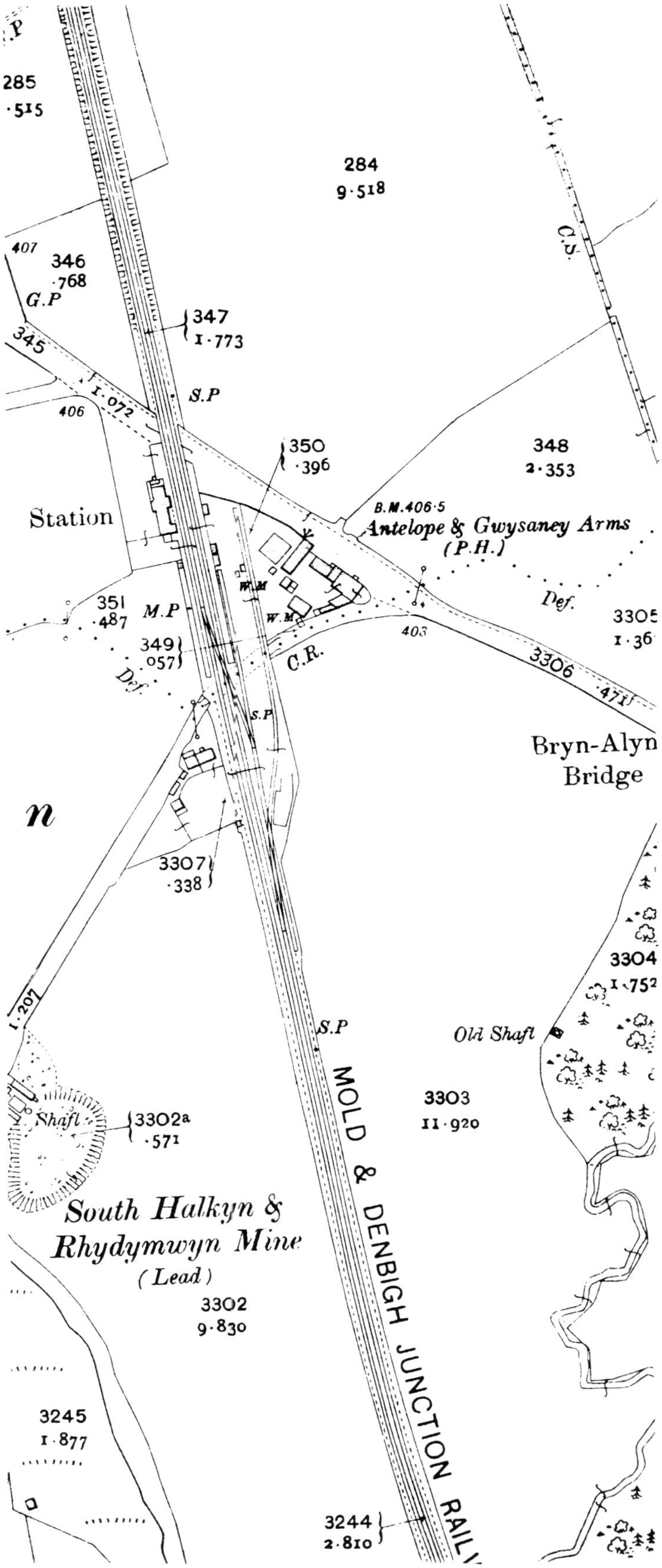
Station
Antelope & Gwysaney Arms
(P.H.)
B.M.406·5
Bryn-Alyn
Bridge
Old Shaft
Shaft
South Halkyn &
Rhydymwyn Mine
(Lead)
MOLD & DENBIGH JUNCTION RAIL
C.R.
C.S.
S.P
M.P
G.P
Def.
W.M
284
9·518
348
2·353
3303
11·920
3302
9·830
3304
3305
3306

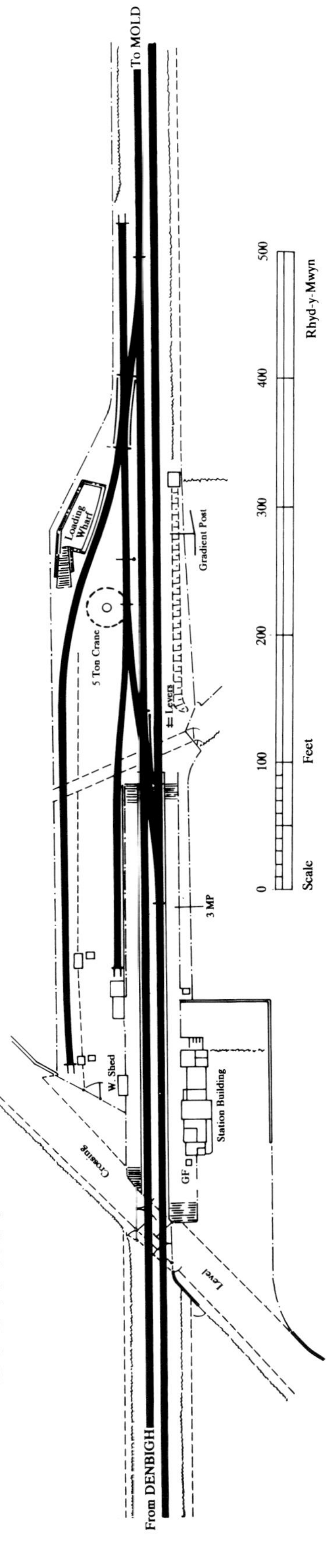
To MOLD
From DENBIGH
Loading Wharf
5 Ton Crane
Gradient Post
Levers
3 MP
W. Shed
Station Building
GF
Crossing
Level
Scale
Feet
Rhyd-y-Mwyn
0
100
200
300
400
500

RHYDYMWYN

108. Rhydymwyn. 23rd April 1959. The Up platform at Rhydymwyn was in keeping with others on the line, although the amount of traffic using the station necessitated providing more oil lamps than at some stations. Beyond the waiting shelter can be seen a small warehouse. Past that is a small ramp, used, it is believed, to load milk churns onto road lorries. Over the fence was the station goods yard, used mainly by local coal merchants. Just visible in the distance is Rhydymwyn Signal Box in this view from a Chester to Denbigh train. *R.J. Buckley.*

109. Rhydymwyn. 5th May 1961. Another view of the Up platform, this time taken from the down side, and showing the main station building. The goods facilities on the Up side were greatly enlarged during World War II when a Ministry of Defence establishment was developed on the Down side of the line. This necessitated the provision of increased sorting and storage facilities on both sides of the line for this traffic. *D. Thompson.*

110. Rhydymwyn. 22nd April 1957. For several years after the war, it was the practice to run a Rambler's Excursion train on Easter Mondays, organised by the Merseyside Ramblers Association. A seven coach special train was run from Birkenhead to Denbigh, and the walkers were set down at various points for an enjoyable day out, being picked up in the evening at various locations along the line. Here, a substantial 'invasion' descends on Rhydymwyn, and patiently wait to give up their tickets at the barrier, whilst the train proceeds on towards Denbigh. Note the sleepers stacked on the Down platform and the rails in the 4ft on the Up side, for track renewal work. *W.A. Camwell.*

111. Rhydymwyn. n.d. Taken from a Chester to Denbigh train as it pulls away from the station across the level crossing. The platform staff discuss some topic as they extract a barrow from its usual parking place, surveyed by an interested spectator looking over the fence close to a bi-lingual trespass warning notice. The poster board lists the train times and also the special Cheap Day fare to Chester, price 3/7d (18p). The Dolfechlas Crossing Distant signal arm is drooping somewhat; either the ground frame lever has just been released, and the arm is dropping, or more likely, the signal wire has expanded.
Author's Collection.

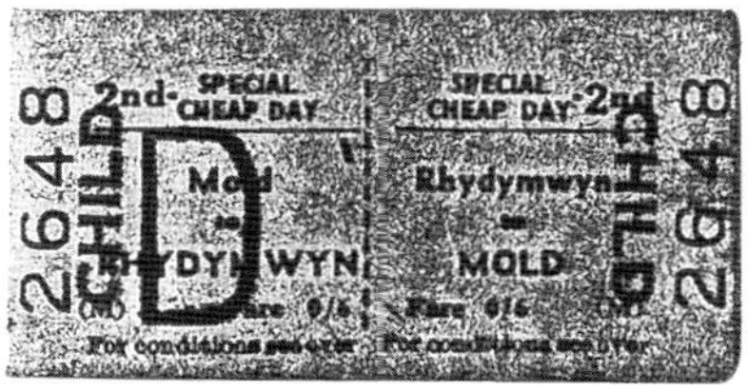

112. Alyn Tin-Plate Signal Box. 18th September 1961. One mile towards Denbigh from Mold station was Alyn Tin-Plate Signal Box, located on the Up side. The Alyn Steel Tin-Plate works had closed some time previously, but Synthite Ltd., a Chemical manufacturer, had created a works almost opposite the box and their traffic justified the box's retention, although latterly it was only switched in as required. Perhaps this is the reason the windows were protected by wire mesh, to discourage vandalism. Here, a Denbigh bound train passes the signal box.
D.S. Foulkes Roberts.

113. Mold. 18th September 1961. A Ruthin to Chester train approaches Mold, passing under a footbridge (No.3) about 200 yards from Mold station. Today, the Mold by-pass road crosses the former track bed at this point. The abutments of Bridge No.2., which carried the Mold to Sychdyn and Alltami road over the track, are coming into view. Today, the fields are built over. *D.S. Foulkes Roberts.*

114. Mold. 9th May 1949. Class 4P 4-4-0 Compound No.**41162** of Chester shed (6A) stands at Mold Down platform with the 5.42pm Chester to Denbigh working. Whilst this class were not unknown on the line, the normal motive power in regular use was Class 2P 4-4-0's. The Up platform canopy extended the full width of the platform, concealed much of the brickwork, giving the platform a gloomy appearance on all but the sunniest of days. Notice the old style station name-board. The ground disk signal was for the trailing crossover which enabled locomotives to run round the stock when trains terminated at Mold. *E.S. Russell.*

Mold

As mentioned elsewhere, Mold station was the terminus of the line from Saltney Ferry, as authorised by the Mold Railway, and also on completion of the Mold & Denbigh Junction Railway, when through running was effected by the two lines meeting at an end-on junction. Whilst the Mold Railway was incorporated into the LNWR, the M&DJR remained nominally independent until the Grouping of 1923.

On the Denbigh side, some 1559 yards before Mold station was reached, the line passed Alyn Tin Plate Works signal box, located on the Up side of the line, and which served a works on the Down side which had disappeared before the second World War. The box was listed in the 1910 register as an LNWR design type 'D' of composite construction, and was 32 years old at that date. It remained in use due to the establishment of Messrs Synthite (Formaldehyde) chemical works on the same site in 1947, and was rail-connected. They had their own four-wheel battery electric shunting locomotive for internal use for many years, but rail traffic had dwindled before the line lost its passenger traffic. The signal box was switched-in as required on weekdays.

The line passed under two road bridges before running into the station. The main station building, constructed of red brick, was on the Down side, with road access from Chester Road, the station being conveniently located for the town and country buses, which terminated and started on Chester Street bridge. Passengers crossed from the Down to the Up side by means of a semi-covered footbridge, a standard Crewe type made of components emanating from the Locomotive Department foundry. The Up platform was somewhat restricted in width at the Denbigh end, and the canopy shielded much of the light to the platform, giving it a gloomy appearance, whilst at the Chester end, the width was more generous, and was of a different style, this part possibly being constructed for the original Mold Railway. On the Down

115. Mold. January 1962. BR Standard Class 4 4-6-0 No.**75033**, based at Mold Junction (6B), pulls away from Mold station with a Chester to Denbigh train of non corridor stock. This view was taken from Chester Bridge - (Bridge No.1.) - on a cold and frosty morning, which emphasised the steam escaping from the carriage heating pipes. Notice the allotments on the side of the track, tended by Mold platform and permanent way staff. The second bridge carries the Mold to Sychdyn/Alltam road over the line. *W.G. Rear.*

side, No.1. siding line was extended and passed in front of the signal cabin to a carriage landing built into the platform. The 1910 list of signal boxes shows the cabin to be of all-brick construction, measuring 18ft x 12ft., and controlled 8 points and 13 signals. It was then 35 years old, and had a predicted life of a further 65 years. A trailing connection off the Down line was made to connect with Price's Siding, as the carriage landing line was known. Latterly, this line was used for timber traffic and also served as a headshunt for the five Down side sidings. Down direction trains could be admitted to No.1. siding at Tryddyn Junction.

On the Up side at the Chester end, three sidings connected with the Up Main line in a trailing direction. The 'Old Denbigh' siding terminated at a set of stops at the platform ramp. The Warehouse Road passed through the building and extended behind the Up side platform, whilst the Horse Landing led off the Warehouse Road. A line from the Up Side shunting neck led back through the shed road and connected with the Horse Landing. Two sidings led off the shed road, one formerly serving Broncoed Colliery. The 1929 Handbook of Railway Stations list the following private sidings which connected with Bromfield Hall Siding (formerly Broncoed Colliery Siding):

R.S. Davies (Bromfield Saw Mills), J.A. Hughes, Thos. Jones, Mold Gas & Water Company, Shell-Mex Ltd., whilst off Mold Argoed Siding, which connected with the horse landing siding, connections were made to Messrs Parry & Co., and Mold Urban District Council.

The signal cabin on the Down side was replaced by a modern structure with flat roof, and contained a Standard $4^1/_2$" centre frame of 35 levers.

There were two trailing crossovers, one of which was located at the Denbigh end of the platform roads, the other located near the signal cabin, and which also gave access to the Up side sidings via a single slip point.

555 yards from Mold station towards Chester, was Tryddyn Junction signal box, similar in size and design to Mold station box and built at the same time. It controlled the junction with the Coed Talon and Brymbo line, as well as the minor road level crossing. The building was an all brick construction, housing a 24 lever LNW Tumbler frame. In the 1910 list this controlled 14 points and 10 signals, but by 1962 this was reduced to 11 working levers. The level crossing gates were controlled from the cabin.

Some passenger trains terminated at Mold, and made use of the station crossover to run round stock. Most frequent users were the trains from Brymbo. Trains from Denbigh made use of the crossover at the Chester end of the station.

The station buildings survived until the mid 1980's, when they were demolished to make way for a new supermarket on the site. After the line closed, the Down side buildings were used as a D.I.Y store.

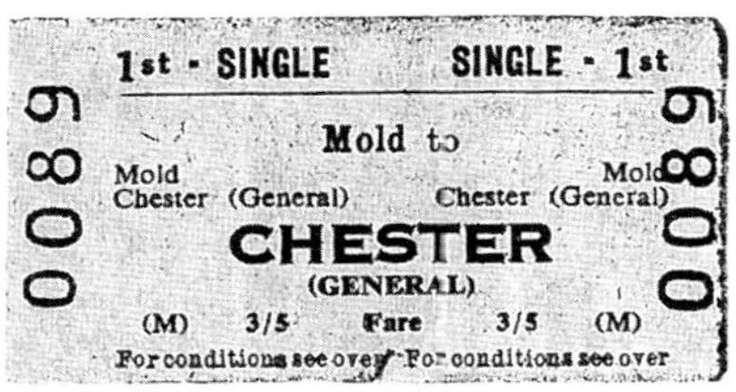

Right: Reproduction from an LMS Handbill for the summer of 1927 giving details of excursion bookings available from Liverpool and stations throughout the Wirral.

To MOLD.

From	Days of Issue.	Outward Trains.			Return Times Day of Issue only.	3rd Class Return Fare.	
		a.m.	a.m.	p.m.		s.	d.
Liverpool (L. Stage) ...	Weekdays	9 20	10 40	1 0		3	8
Birkenhead (W.)	„	9 35	10 55	1 18	Any	3	4
Rock Ferry	„	9 42	11 3	1 26	train after	3	3
Bebington	„	9 35	11 7	1 9	3.0 p.m.	3	2
Spital	„	9 40	11 13	12†50	having	3	0
Bromborough	„	9 44	11 17	12 54	a	2	10
Hooton	„	9 55	11 23	1 18	through	2	8
Ledsham	„	9 36	11 27	1 23	connection.	2	6
Capenhurst	„	9 41	11 32	1 28		2	3
Mollington	„	9 46	11 37	1 33		2	0

S—Saturdays excepted. **SO**—Saturdays only. †—Leaves at 1.33 p.m. Saturdays only.
§—Change at Hooton and proceed at 11.5 a.m. July 16 to August 27 only. **A**—Runs July 16 to August 27 only. **B**—Saturdays only September 3, 10, 17 and 24.

116. Mold. 9th May 1949. LMS Class 4F 0-6-0, renumbered **M4065** whilst in the works for overhaul during the brief period between Nationalisation and the introduction of the permanent re-numbering scheme, between January and April 1948, seen here running around the one coach that was used for the Mold to Brymbo via Coed Talon service. The tender is equipped with coal rails to increase its carrying capacity, a feature not found on every member of the class. Notice the gardens, gas lamp and other platform furniture. The station survived until recently, when it was demolished to make way for a new supermarket. *E.S. Russell.*

117. Mold. 23rd April 1959. Another view of the Up platform looking towards Chester, taken from a Down train as it leaves the station. The platform was somewhat narrow, probably caused by the close proximity of the cottages which were built before the Mold & Denbigh Junction Railway opened its line. *R.J. Buckley.*

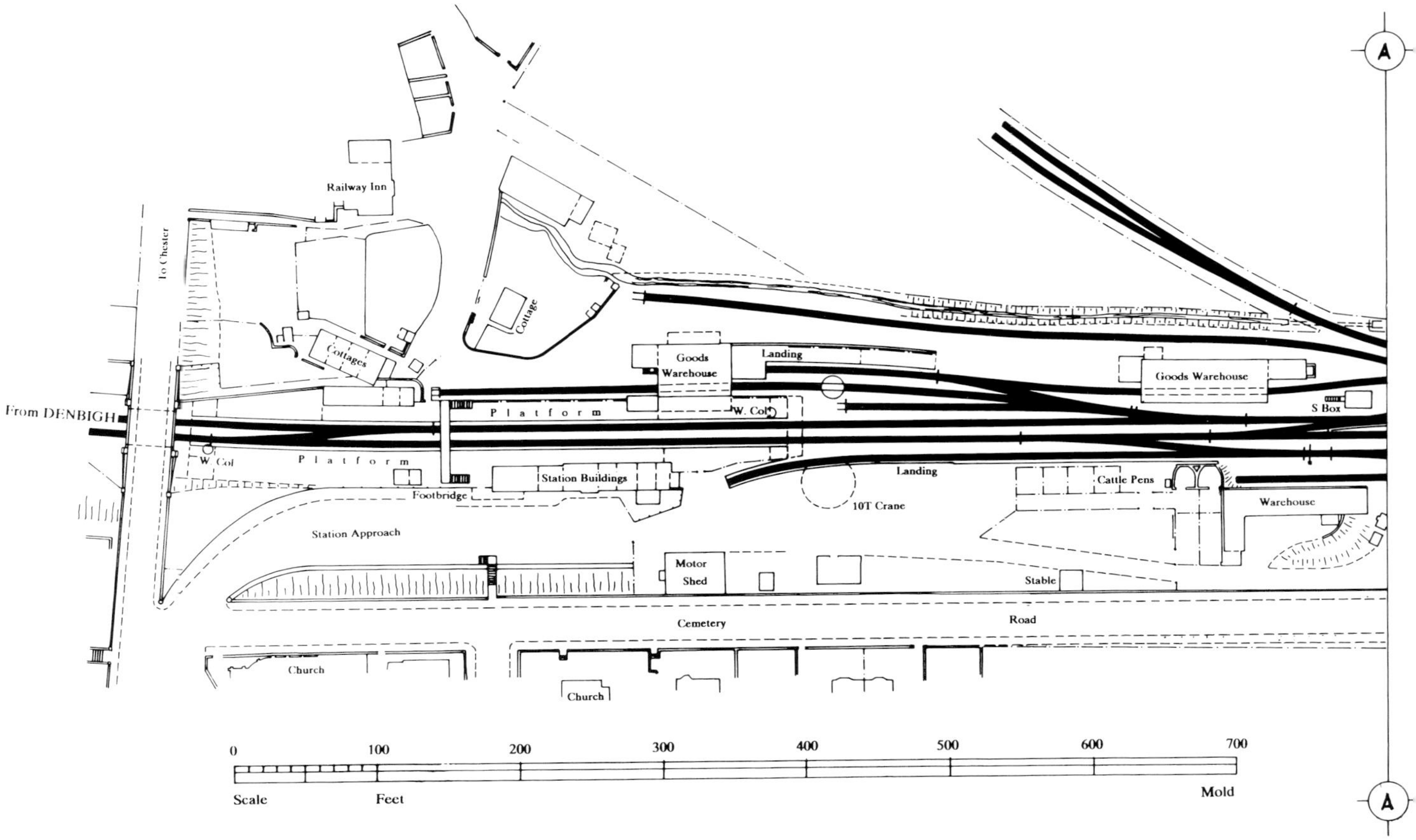

118. Mold. n.d. LNW built Webb design 0-6-2T, believed to be No.**701**, stands in the Down platform with a train to Denbigh, whilst the driver, fireman and guard pose for the picture. The date and photographer are not known, but it would seem likely that this picture was taken around 1923. The loco is distinctly grubby, which would not have been tolerated before the war. On the Up side, a train of coal passes through the platform, although we can only guess where it has come from. *Author's collection.*

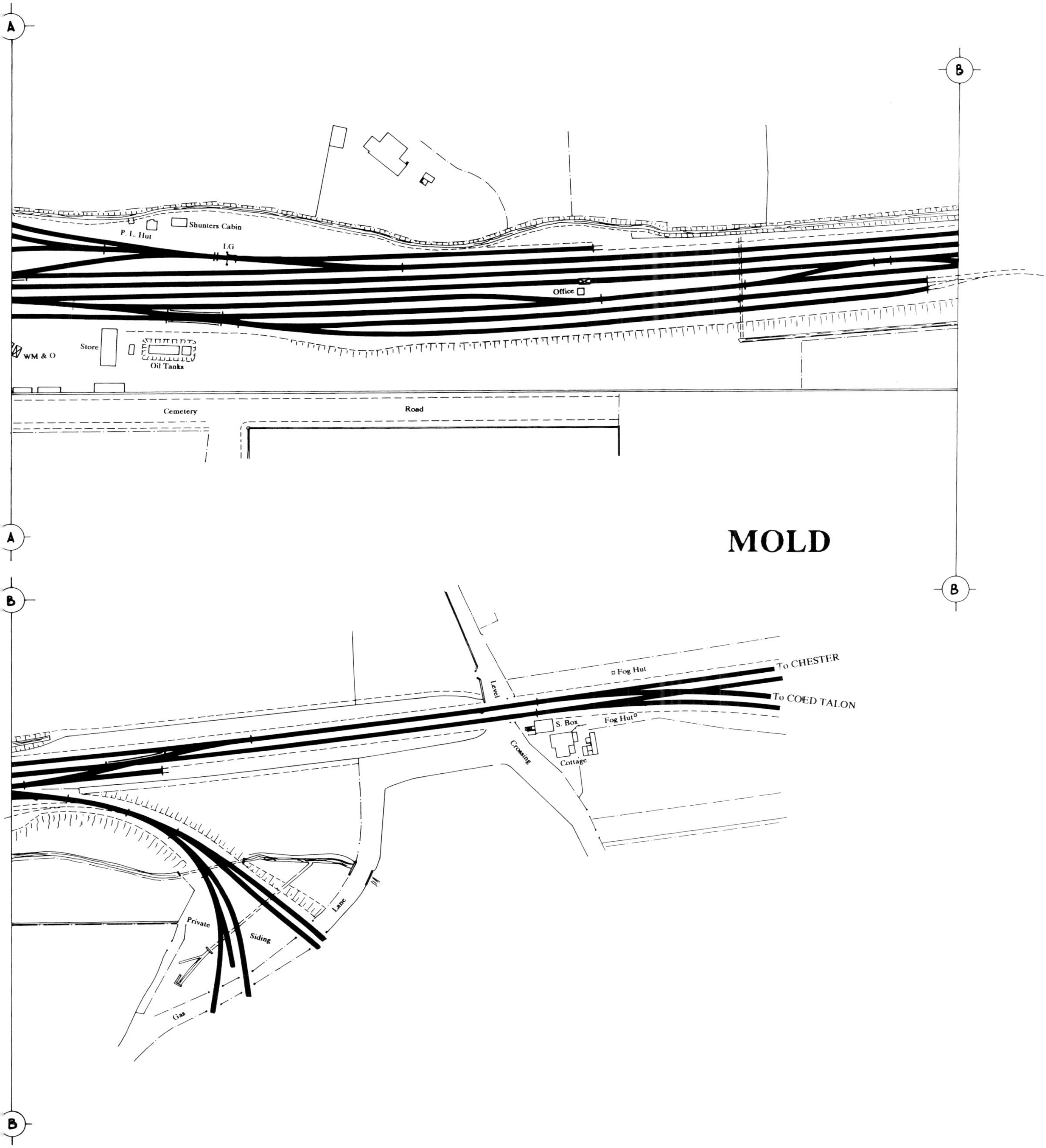
A
B
P. L. Hut
Shunters Cabin
LG
Office
Store
WM & O
Oil Tanks
Cemetery
Road
MOLD
Fog Hut
To CHESTER
To COED TALON
Level
Crossing
S. Box
Fog Hut
Cottage
Lane
Private
Siding
Gas

119. Mold. n.d. Another view of the back of the Crosville Motor Services waiting shelter, taken from the Down platform at Mold station Notice the ornamental flower beds, maintained by the platform staff, and a frequent winner of 'best station gardens' competitions held by the London Midland Region. The station name was picked out in the grass, and the seat carried the station name on its back support. Even the bus shelter supports were whitewashed by the enthusiastic staff! *Author's collection.*

120. Mold. 15th July 1963. Twelve months after passenger traffic to Mold ceased, Class 4F 0-6-0 No.**44595** of Mold Junction shed (6B) pulls into the Down platform. At this time these locomotives worked regularly to Mold and after a period of shunting in the yard, worked a trip to Coed Talon and back, before returning to Mold Junction. In the intervening period, the garden, left to its own devices, has gone wild, . The gas lamps remain, but the platform furniture and the enamel station signs have been removed. The station has taken on an air of depression, which would persist for many more years before the ultimate demolition. *R.M.Casserley.*

121. Mold. 10th September 1959. Stanier 2-6-4T No.**42482** of Chester Shed (6A) pulls into the station with the 4.30pm (Saturdays Only) train from Chester to Ruthin, on what should have been the last Saturday of the summer season. Due to a printer's strike, the time tables could not be printed and an interim service was brought into force the following Monday, although it did not affect the Chester to Denbigh services very much. The time tables finally appeared on 2nd November 1959. There is a good display of posters on view, and including one just visible by the smokebox, which states that a cheap day return to Denbigh cost 3/- (15p). The exhaust steam injector has blown back - a common complaint which occurred when the driver shut the regulator, and the change-over valve, which should have admitted live steam to the injector, failed to pick up. *Norman Jones.*

122. Mold. 14th June 1961. In happier times, BR Standard Class 4 4-6-0 No.**75034** based at Mold Junction (6B) runs into the Down platform with the 1.35pm from Chester to Denbigh, comprising three non corridor coaches. Notice the Up side water tank, and the canopy supports, which were different from those at the Denbigh end of the same platform. The goods yard on the Up side is full of stock, a factor which ensured that the line remained open for freight traffic after the passenger service ceased.
D.S. Foulkes Roberts.

123. Mold. 10th September 1959. An unidentified 2-6-4T pulls into the Up platform at Mold with a Denbigh to Chester working. At this time most trains carried consignments of mail in the guards compartment, to Chester, where it was sorted. On the Down platform, some of the detail can be gleaned from this view. Notice the different style of seat. The usual display of posters adorns the wall boards, whilst standard information signs are suspended from the canopy, with passenger information. *Norman Jones.*

124. Mold. 1961. The independent Mold Railway constructed the line from Saltney Junction to Mold, although it was operated by the LNWR from the commencement of services, and for several years all the passenger traffic was worked from Mold to Chester. An engine shed was built here, but with the opening of the through route to Denbigh, train operation was transferred to Chester and Denbigh, and the former engine shed being converted to a grain warehouse. Nevertheless, the outline of the original engine shed can clearly be seen, as shown in this view. The line passing through the gate to the right of the shed once formed part of the siding to Broncoed Colliery, which provided much mineral traffic in the early days of the line. This view was taken from a private charter DMU that traversed the Coed Talon branch as well as working through to Denbigh and Corwen before returning to Rhyl and back along the coast to Chester, with a minor diversion to Dyserth and back. *G.H. Platt.*

125. Mold. c.1969. Another view of the former engine shed at Mold, together with the former office, taken after the passenger traffic ceased, and towards the end of the line's existence. There is an air of dereliction about the place, although the presence of a van indicates that there is still some traffic along the line. Latterly the rail facilities at Mold were a shadow of their former self, with several tracks in the goods yard being lifted, although both lines through the former passenger platforms survived, as did the station buildings complete with their canopies, until complete closure of the line. The signal box was subsequently demolished and all surviving points were worked from hand levers. Few signals survived, but a fixed distant arm was installed in the Down direction at the ramp of Mold station platform, 600 yards from the barrier level crossing over the new Mold by-pass road. *Author's collection.*

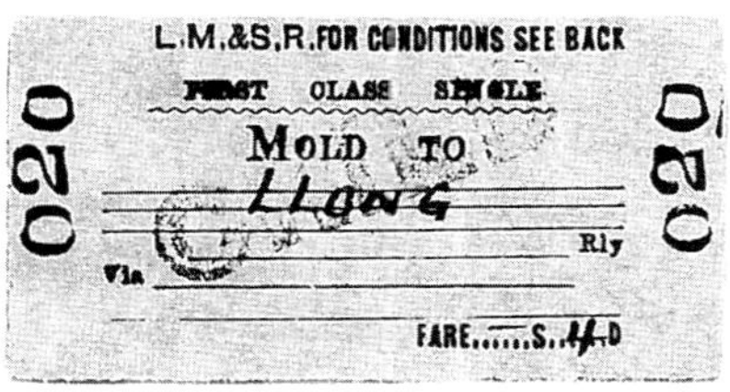

126. Mold - Tryddyn Junction. n.d. Tryddyn Junction signal box was the point where the line to Coed Talon branched off the main line. The box controlled the junction and the level crossing, which was hand operated, and survived until the closure of the branch. This view shows the Coed Talon line forking off right and the double line towards Llong and Chester. The box was manned throughout the day, presumably to attend to the level crossing. It was closed from 3rd March 1965. *Author's collection.*

127. Coed Talon. 1961. The station building at Coed Talon was a grim looking structure, built of local dressed stone, and by all accounts, the house was damp most of the year. The level crossing gates were hand operated by the porter on duty, and were normally closed to rail traffic. The goods yard was always busy, as can be seen from the variety of wagons and vans in the yard, and freight traffic increased slightly after passenger services were withdrawn in 1951. The building on the extreme right of the picture was at one time a smithy, and beyond that was a timber yard and store. Beyond the vans, the track curves away towards Mold. *G.H. Platt.*

Mold to Coed Talon & Brymbo.

The branch from Mold to Coed Talon & Brymbo was jointly owned by the LNWR and GWR, and operated primarily a freight line, although through passenger services survived until 27th March 1950. The LNWR and its successors worked the regular passenger service trains although at one time the GWR operated an early morning and afternoon workmen's train, the stock being parked overnight at Mold, with the loco travelling light before and after working the trip from and to Croes Newydd depot. Latterly the passenger service was confined to two trips each way Mondays to Fridays, and chiefly for children travelling from Coed Talon to Mold Grammar School. Mold Junction engines and men worked the service, latterly the usual motive power for the single coach working being a 6B Fowler 4F 0-6-0. In between the passenger trips engine and men worked the freight trips on the branch and shunted at Mold in between workings. The first set of men worked a Class 'K' freight train to Mold early morning and after depositing the wagons in the sidings, picked up the single coach for the return passenger trip. Relieving and relieved train crews travelled out and home as passengers, the second set of men working back to the depot with a Class 'K' freight working in the early evening.

Coed Talon station provided the main source of passenger traffic, limited though that was, with the main revenue for the station and the line coming from freight traffic.

There were no Sunday services on the branch, although occasionally excursion trains were worked according to requirements. Most popular destination for such traffic was to Rhyl, via Denbigh.

The line was single throughout, with token sections from Tryddyn Junction to Coed Talon (4 miles 498 yards), and Coed Talon to Brymbo (4 miles 176 yards). Intermediate stations were provided at Coed Talon, Llanfynydd and Ffrith. At Brymbo the GW Station was shared, but under the control of the GWR.

The 1910 signal box list shows an 8ft x 8ft all wood structure at Coed Talon, housing a frame which controlled 10 points and 7 signals. Latterly the single line token equipment was kept in the Station office at Coed Talon, with the 8 lever frame (5 working) on the platform being exposed to the elements. Single platforms sufficed at the intermediate stations with very basic shelter. There were no signals provided at Llanfynydd or Ffrith. At Llanfynydd a small two lever ground frame controlled access to a single siding on the Down side that served as a goods yard which could hold 3 wagons. A small yard crane was provided. Between the two halts were Crown Dale and Trimley Hall Colliery sidings, both on the Up side. Between Ffrith and Brymbo were Glascoed Siding and Bwlchgwyn sidings on the Up side and Prince of Wales sidings on the Down beyond Glascoed level crossing.

In 1952 the section from Coed Talon to Brymbo was closed completely and the track lifted. No photographs have been located of Llanfynydd or Ffrith stations when the line was open.

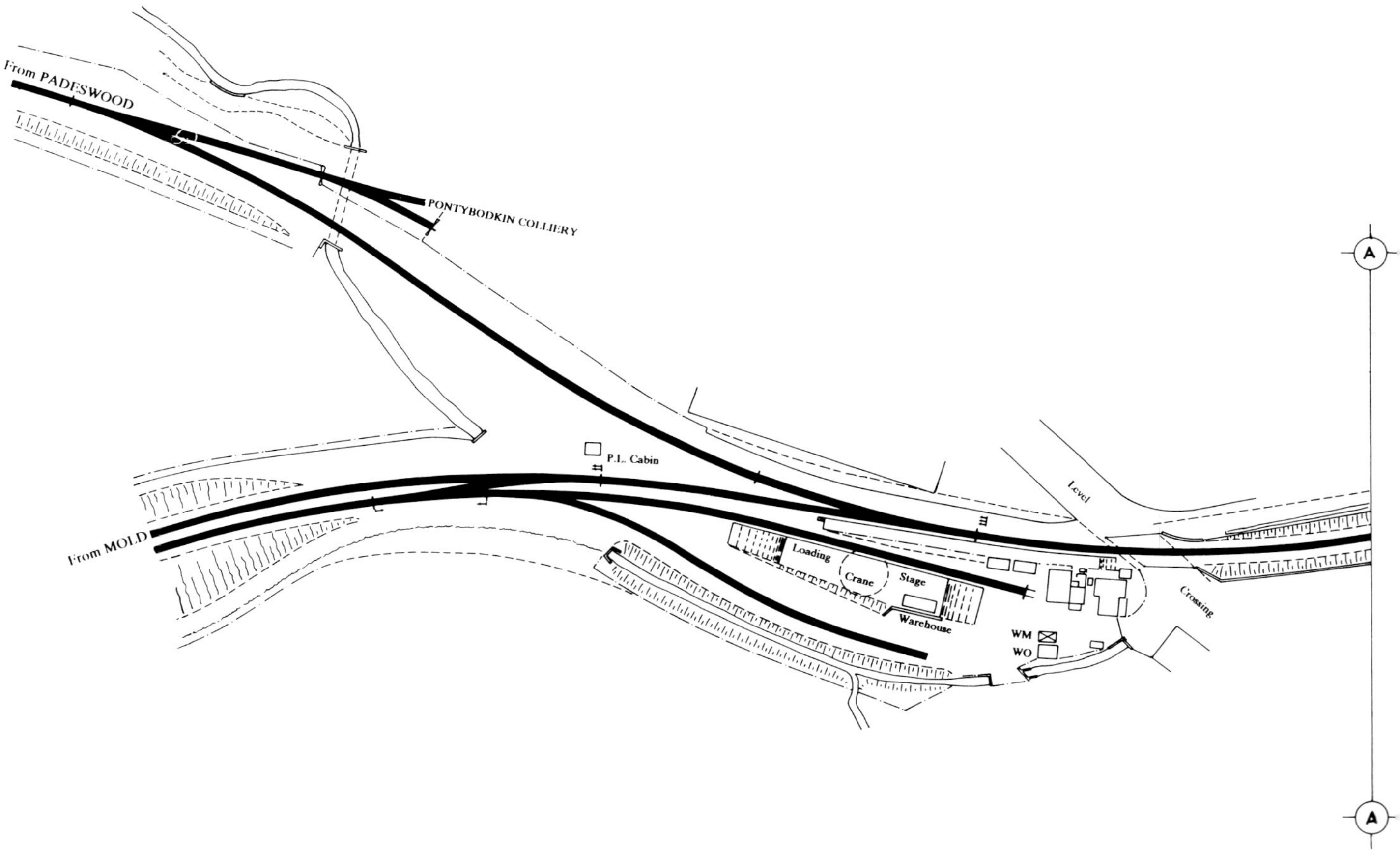
From PADESWOOD
PONTYBODKIN COLLIERY
P.L. Cabin
From MOLD
Loading
Crane
Stage
Warehouse
Level
Crossing
WM
WO
A
A

128 (left). **Coed Talon. c.1950.** Coed Talon station consisted of a single platform with a stone built house for the Station master, a brick built Booking Office together with a wooden waiting room and store. The goods yard sat astride the line, with a small yard crane behind the platform. The line at this point was bisected by the Mold to Tryddyn road, and the level crossing gates were hand operated. This view shows the station before regular passenger trains to Brymbo had ceased. *L&GRP No.23575*

129 (right). **Coed Talon. 1961.** The line from Tryddyn Junction on the Chester to Mold line approached Coed Talon in this cutting, the right hand track being the running line. Access to the goods yard was off the loop, formed by the left hand line. The line was mainly used for freight traffic, although for many years school children travelled from here to Mold to attend the Grammar School. *G.H. Platt.*

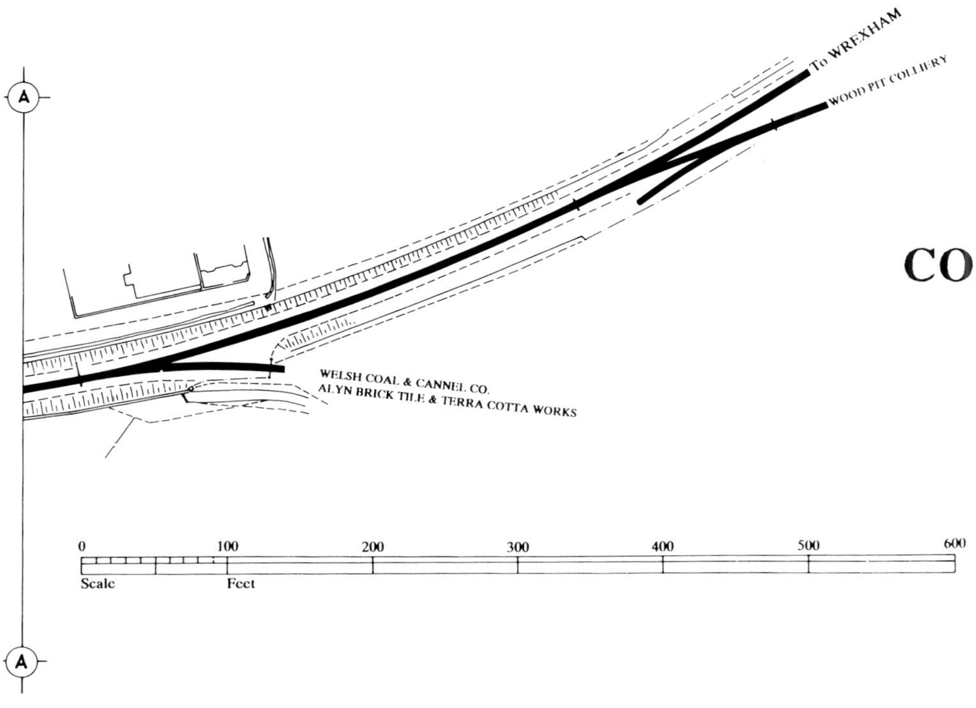

COED TALON

130. Brymbo. 9th May 1949. Photographs of LM Region trains at Brymbo are extremely rare. Here, Mold Junction shed's Fowler 0-6-0 No.**M4065** with its one coach awaits departure time. Passenger traffic was usually confined to carrying the schoolchildren between Coed Talon and Mold in the morning and returning them after school. The service didn't run on Saturdays. Note the exposed situation of the station, perched on the hillside opposite the Steelworks. The wooden building was in poor condition, and traffic did not justify retaining the services. The Western Region also worked into this station, but only freight traffic from and to Wrexham, having ceased operating passenger trains to Brymbo in 1931. LM Region passenger services finished on 27th March 1950. *E.S. Russell.*

131. Coed Talon. 1961. Possibly the only time a DMU worked into Coed Talon was the SLS Special Railtour which traversed the line from Chester to Denbigh and Corwen as well as diverting at Tryddyn Junction for this unique occasion. Here, the four coach unit waits, partly in the short platform, whilst the photographs are taken, before reversing to pick up the itinerary at Mold. *G.H. Platt.*

132. Llong. 22nd April 1957. Most of the station buildings on the Mold Railway were a uniform design, and similar to the smaller station buildings on the Chester & Holyhead main line, designed by Francis Thompson. Here it was located on the Down side and survives to this day. The platforms were low and relatively short in length. The level crossing was hand operated, and signals were controlled from a ten lever frame mounted on the platform, visible behind the station nameboard. *W.A. Camwell.*

Llong

The station was 1 mile 55 chains from Mold, with the main station buildings located on the Down side. These were of uniform design to others built for the Mold Railway, and similar to the smaller stations designed by the same architect for the Chester & Holyhead Railway. The Mold Railway stations were built with very low height platforms and Llong was no exception. A minor road level crossing bisected the line at the Chester end, and at one time a signal cabin of composite construction, to LNWR pattern 'F', stood on the Down side beyond the crossing. This controlled 6 points and 7 signals. Sidings were located on the Up side but these were removed in the 1930's, with the signal box being abolished at the same time. An eight lever frame was mounted on the Down platform, which controlled the gate lock and signals. The Up platform had a general waiting room and ladies waiting room and toilets provided, passengers booking their tickets on the Down side and then crossing to the Up platform by means of the level crossing. The station was isolated from any community, on a minor road, and passenger traffic was sufficiently sparse to justify the station's temporary closure from 1st January 1917 until 5th May 1919 as a wartime economy measure. Despite this, the station remained open to passenger traffic until passenger services were withdrawn in 1962.

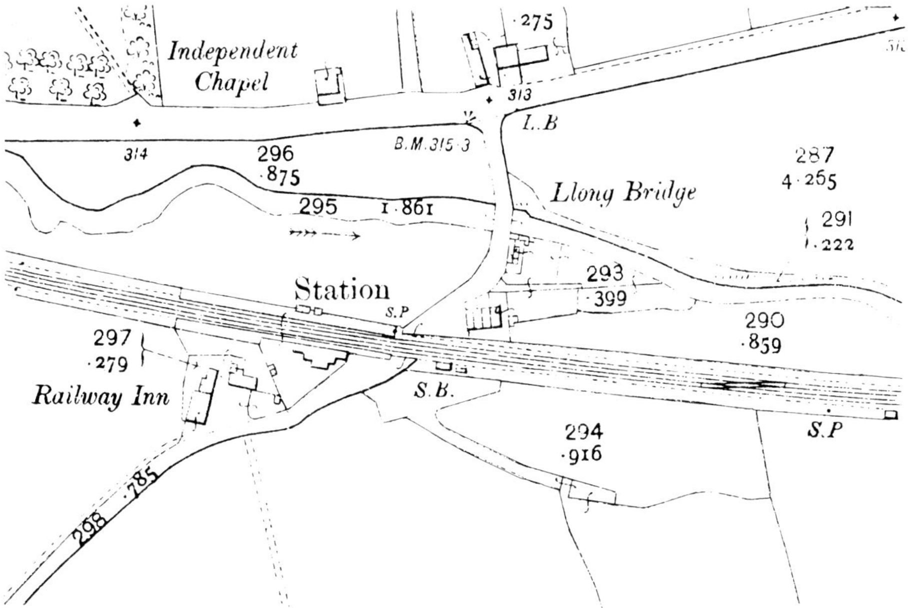

133. Llong. 23rd April 1959. The Up platform at Llong was a simple structure, edged with slabs, and compressed soil infill. An open fronted waiting shelter was provided, with a separate Ladies Waiting Room close by, and at the Chester end of the platform. The level crossing continued to be hand operated. This view shows these features, taken from a Chester to Denbigh train. Also visible is the trailing crossover beyond the level crossing. *R.J. Buckley.*

LLONG

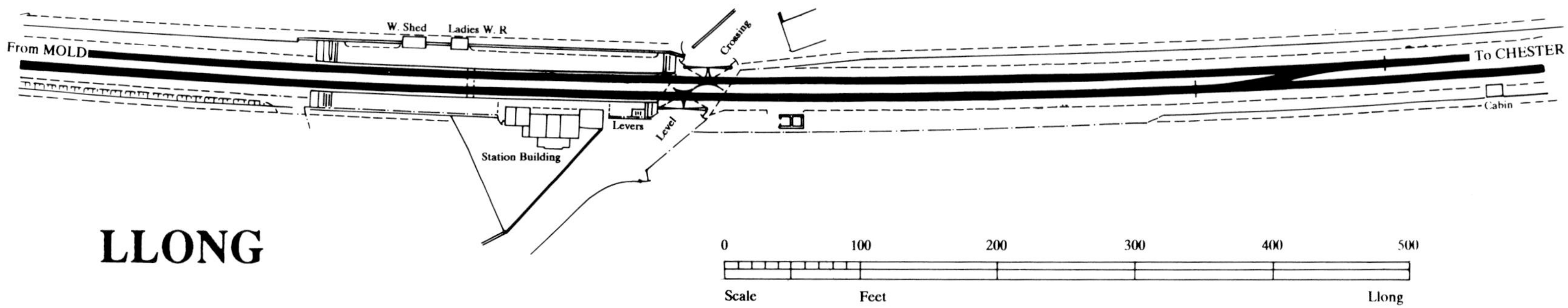

134. Llong. n.d. The signal box at Llong was of composite construction, LNWR standard pattern 'F' model located on the Down side. It was not replaced when falling due for renewal, and a platform mounted ten lever frame was located on the Down platform superceded it. Notice the Up starter, with the spectacle mounted separately and below the level of the signal arm. The platforms were low and latterly, portable steps were provided to assist passengers boarding and alighting. *C. Dawson collection.*

135. Llong. n.d. In LNWR days, points and signals were controlled from a standard composite signal cabin, located on the Down side at the Chester end of the level crossing. This general view shows the box in the settlement around the station, and in addition to controlling the signals and level crossing gates, at one time a siding existed on the Up side together with a trailing crossover, which were controlled from the fifteen lever frame. The crossover survived until the line lost its passenger services. *C.Dawson collection.*

Padeswood & Buckley

The station building design was the exception to those built for the Mold Railway, and the offices were located astride the line, with steps down from the booking office to the platforms below. The station was 10 miles 59 chains from Chester General Station and 2 mile 46 chains from Mold. The platforms were of low height and somewhat shorter than usual. Geographically it was some distance from Buckley, and not very close to Padeswood either, a factor which might have hastened its complete closure, somewhat earlier than the other stations, from 6th January 1958. The station buildings were demolished almost immediately after closure and the platforms had been removed by early 1959. At one time there was a small goods yard on the Down side, with a goods shed and two sidings, controlled from a small ground frame.

Beyond the station was Padeswood Junction, at one time called Ffrith Junction, where the freight only Ffrith branch to Coed Talon branched off on the Down side, controlled by Padeswood Junction signal box, a Standard LNW design box of type 'E' and of composite construction, which housed a lever frame controlling 11 points and 13 signals. This branch closed completely in 1934 and the signal box was removed at the same time.

A short distance further on towards Chester, on the Up side, was the Padeswood Colliery branch junction. There is no reference to the colliery in the July 1904 working time table and it is assumed that the colliery had ceased working by this date.

136. Padeswood & Buckley. 22nd April 1957. The Up platform at Padeswood, looking back towards Mold. Passengers descended a flight of stairs from the booking hall to platform level. Apart from an open waiting shelter, there was little accommodation available, and the whole station presented a somewhat dismal encounter for the passenger. The matching platform shelters and facilities were somewhat sparse in comfort, but passenger traffic was equally so. Exactly why the station building was so constructed remains a mystery. The Station Master lived in a cottage close by, and not 'over the shop'. The platforms have an unkempt air about them, and it is assumed that the decision to close the station completely was already made known to staff, hence the abandoned flower beds that used to adorn the platforms. *W.A. Camwell.*

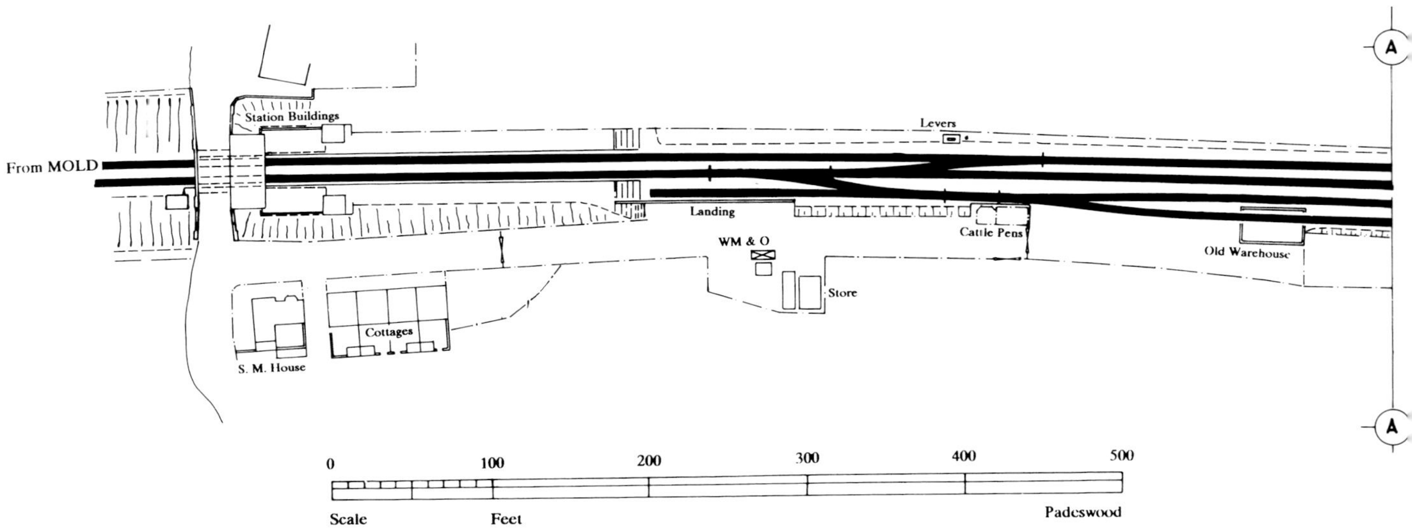

137. Padeswood. n.d. Padeswood & Buckley station about 1900, showing the goods yard and warehouse on the Down side. Beyond the goods shed, the freight only 'Coppa' branch to Coed Talon passed in front of the Providence Iron Works, whose chimneys can be seen near the right hand edge of the picture. In the distance, on the Up side, is Padeswood signal cabin, which was a standard LNW size 'E' box of composite construction, which controlled 11 points and 13 signals. With the closure of the Coppa branch, following the accident at Pontblyddyn in 1935, the line was lifted and presumably the box was closed and removed about this time. *C. Dawson collection.*

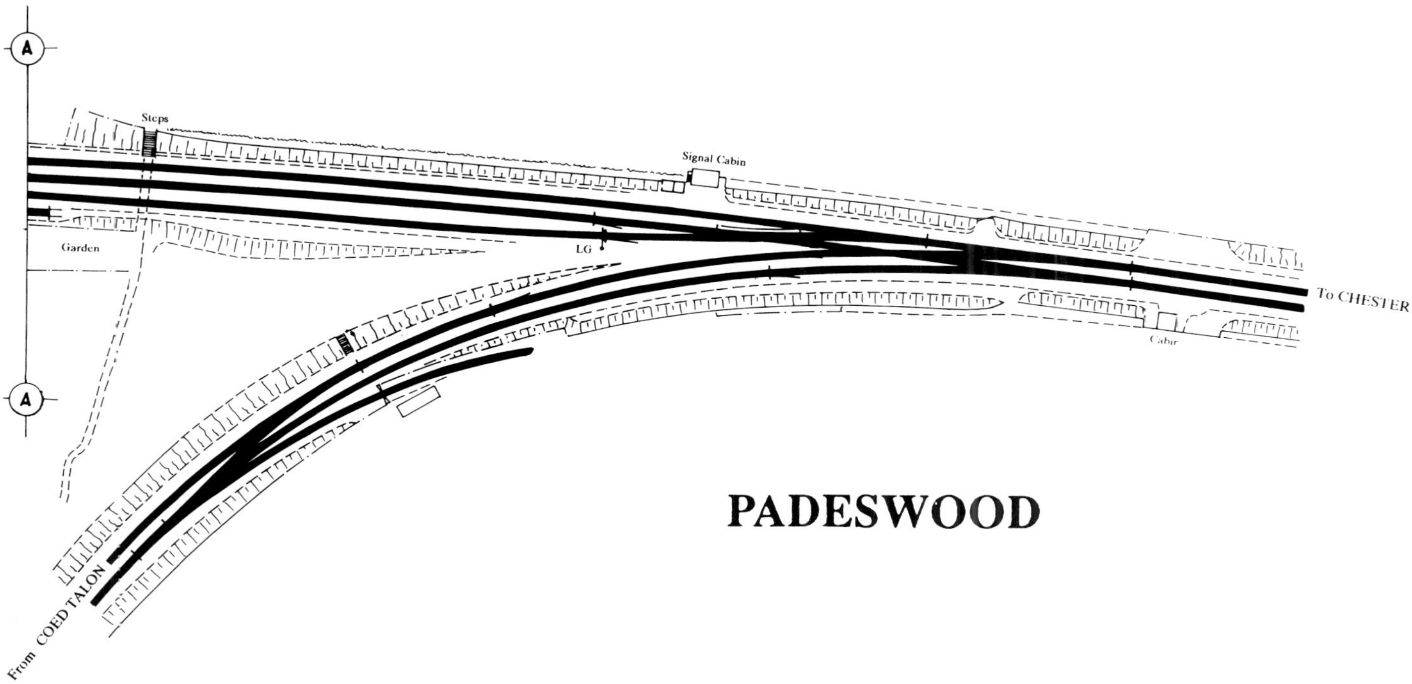

PADESWOOD

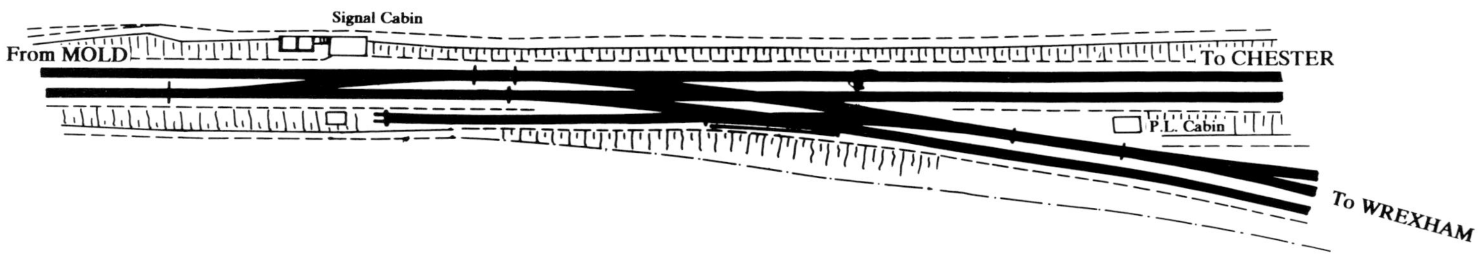

138. **Hope Junction. 1960.** There was considerable exchange traffic between the LNWR/LMS and the WMCQR/GCR/LNER, mostly mineral traffic coming from the coalfield in the Wrexham area. A double line spur from the Wrexham to Bidston line descended to the Chester to Mold line on the Down side, with additional siding capacity that ran parallel to the spur lines. Here, a Denbigh to Chester train approaches the junction. An unidentified BR Standard Class 9F 2-10-0 waits in the distance, with a train of mineral wagons. *G.H. Platt.*

139. **Hope Junction. 1960.** Another view of the spur line to the WM&CQR, this time taken from a Chester to Denbigh train. In addition to the open mineral wagon, some 'Presflo' wagons, used for cement powder traffic, can be seen amongst the raft of wagons, bound, no doubt, for Tunnel cement Works at Padeswood. Traffic from this works along this spur line is all that now remains of the line. *G.H. Platt.*

140. Hope Exchange Low Level. 10th July 1948. Fowler 0-6-0 Class 4F No.**M4065** pauses at Hope Exchange platform with a Chester to Denbigh train. There seems a scarcity of passengers, which was not unusual, but the guard is unloading some parcel traffic, which the porter on duty will have to carry to the High level station across the fields. *W.A. Camwell.*

Hope Junction & Hope Exchange

One mile from Padeswood & Buckley station was Hope Junction, where freight traffic was exchanged with the LNER line from Wrexham to Connah's Quay, Chester Northgate and Seacombe. Traffic from the LMS to the LNER line was worked from Mold Junction and set back from the Down line into the exchange sidings. In the reverse direction, locomotives were utilised to assist freight trains up Kinnerton bank, and were detached at Hope Junction, where they would pick up a return working to Mold Junction. Most of the traffic dealt with was coal from the Wrexham pits. Not all workings were shown in the Working Time Table, but were listed in the Shunting & Trip Engine Workings for Chester District. Upon Nationalisation, the LNER line passed into London Midland Region control but the exchange working persisted as formerly. Traffic was controlled from Hope Junction signal box, which was a standard LNWR design cabin, type 'E', of composite construction, located on the Up side. In the 1910 list it was shown as having a 27 lever tumbler frame with 19 working levers, of which nos. 5,7,8,9,15,21,22 and 23 were spare.

Hope Exchange station, renamed Hope Exchange Low Level from 7th December 1953, was 1 mile 34 chains from Padeswood station, some distance away from Hope village, and served as a convenient point for passengers to change to and from the LNER line. There was no roadway connecting the stations, merely a footpath, and the platforms had very basic accommodation. There were no freight facilities here, although a porter was in attendance for part of the day to deal with any parcels interchange. Most passenger trains called at the station, but traffic was always light and it closed to traffic on 1st September 1958.

141. Hope Exchange Low Level. 23rd April 1959. The short Up platform at the Low Level station comprised a small office and separate waiting shed, together with a permanent way hut on the platform, with similar facilities on the Down platform. There was no road access, the platforms merely a convenient point where passengers could transfer to and from the Wrexham to Bidston line. Connection was by a footpath over the fields, and traffic, as might be expected, was minimal. *R.J. Buckley.*

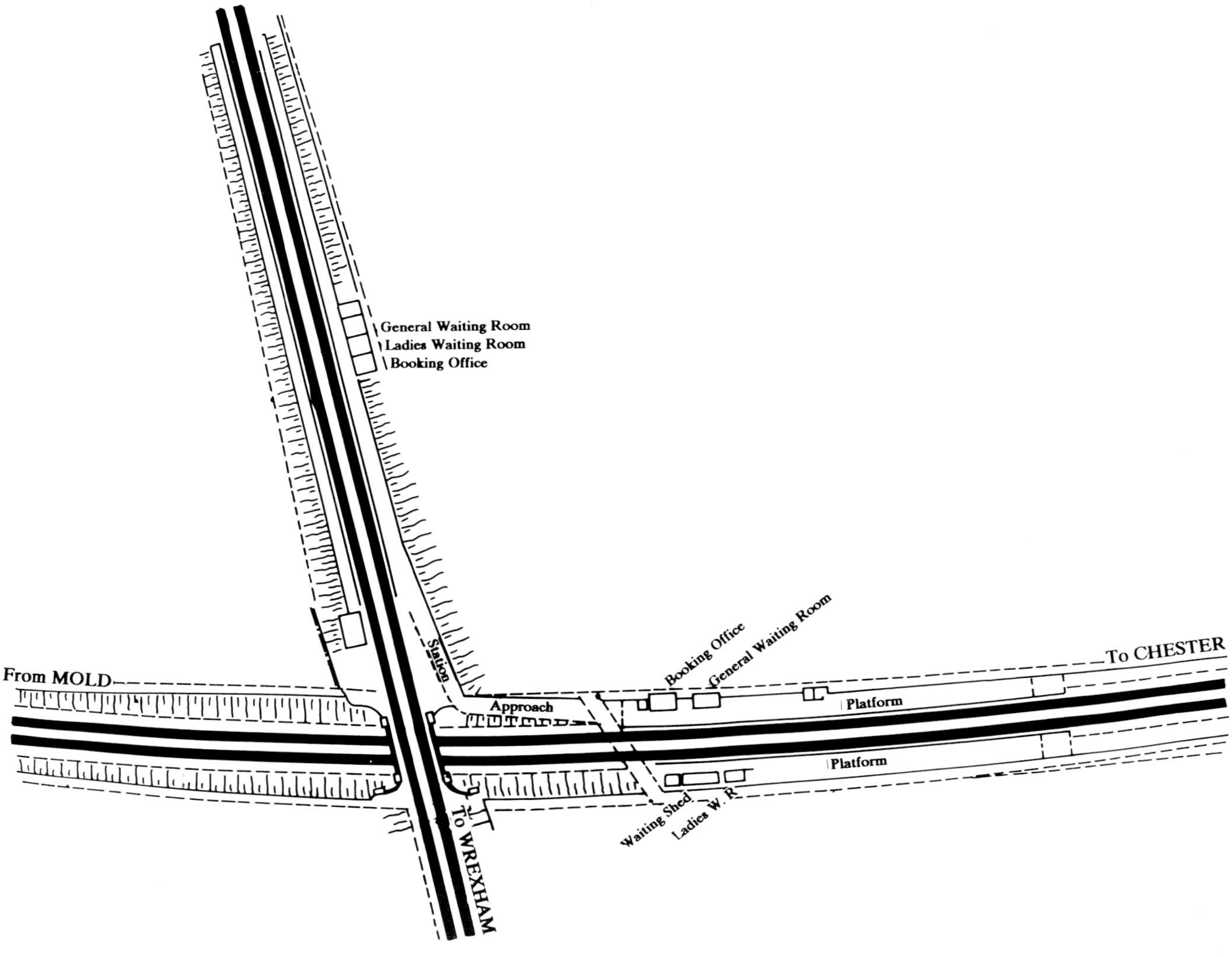

142. Hope & Penyffordd. 22nd April 1957. The Fowler 2-6-2T engines were rarely seen on the Denbigh to Chester services, indeed few members of this class were active in the area, although both Llandudno Junction and Bangor had diagrammed turns for them. No.**40060** was transferred to Rhyl (6K) shed on 9th March, and spent most of its days shunting at Rhyl, but was allowed out on certain occasions. On this day it worked to Denbigh and then took over the 12.46pm to Chester, seen here awaiting departure time. The gates had been closed after the train had cleared the crossing, and after a few more minutes wait, continued on its journey to Chester. *W.A. Camwell.*

Hope & Penyffordd

The station was actually located in Penyffordd village, and was nine miles from Chester and four and three quarter miles from Mold. The station buildings were on the Down side and were uniform with most other stations on the Mold Railway. The Up platform had a waiting shelter which offered some protection against the elements. A footbridge straddled the line adjoining the level crossing. The A550 Queensferry to Wrexham road crossed the line on the level, the gates being worked from the signal box which stood on the Up side, adjacent to the crossing. Trailing sidings led off both running lines on the Mold side of the station, with a trailing crossover on the running lines. A third siding was located on the Down side before the platform. Originally an LNWR all brick signal cabin measuring 28' 6" x 14' 0" controlling 11 points and 9 signals was provided, but this was replaced about 1943 on the same site by an LMS design 'ARP' version with flat roof. The frame was replaced at the same time by an LMS tappet frame with 25 levers. The two sidings on the Down side were taken out after the war. There was some commuter traffic from Penyffordd to both Chester and Mold and the community protested strongly when the proposal to withdraw passenger services was made. Freight traffic was withdrawn from 5th September 1955.

143. Hope & Penyffordd. 1947. The main buildings at Hope & Penyffordd station were on the Down side, and were of the same uniform design as many of the other stations on the Mold Railway. The modern 'ARP' design signal box controls the level crossing and the sidings beyond the crossing. Notice the tall lower quadrant Down Home signal. The station is adorned with 'Astons' enamel signs, in common with most stations in North Wales. Notice also the bracket signal for the Up line, and the gas lamp mounted on the footbridge. *D. Thompson.*

144. Hope & Penyffordd. 23rd April 1959. The Up platform shelter was perhaps a bit more lavish than some on the Chester to Denbigh line, and may have been an alternative to the usual wooden structures seen elsewhere. The staff here always took immense pride in their gardens and the flowerbeds extending along the platform show their dedication in this respect. *R.J. Buckley.*

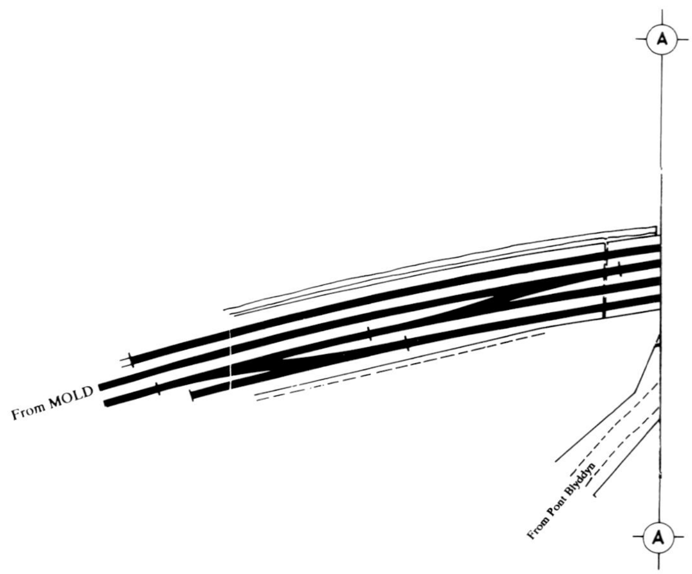

145. Hope & Penyffordd. 7th August 1948. Class 4P 4-4-0 Compound No.**1098**, of Chester (6A) shed stands at the Up platform with the 2.25pm from Corwen to Chester. These engines were not unknown on the Corwen service, but generally their services were in demand on the North Wales coast main line, and could not be spared for mundane three coach local workings. The fireman is more intent on watching the photographer, and his exhaust injector is discharging water onto the track. The length of the round trip demanded that a tender engine be rostered, and it was the practice to turn the engine at Denbigh on the outward journey and work tender first to Corwen, so that the through return working could be undertaken with the smokebox leading. Among the buildings located on the Down platform at Hope & Penyffordd was the Ladies Waiting Room, which was a small wooden building, a short distance apart from the main building, which housed a General Waiting Room, the Booking Office and Booking Hall. Passengers were supposed to cross the line by the footbridge, but in practice it was quicker and less exhausting to use the roadway and cross on the level. *W.A. Camwell.*

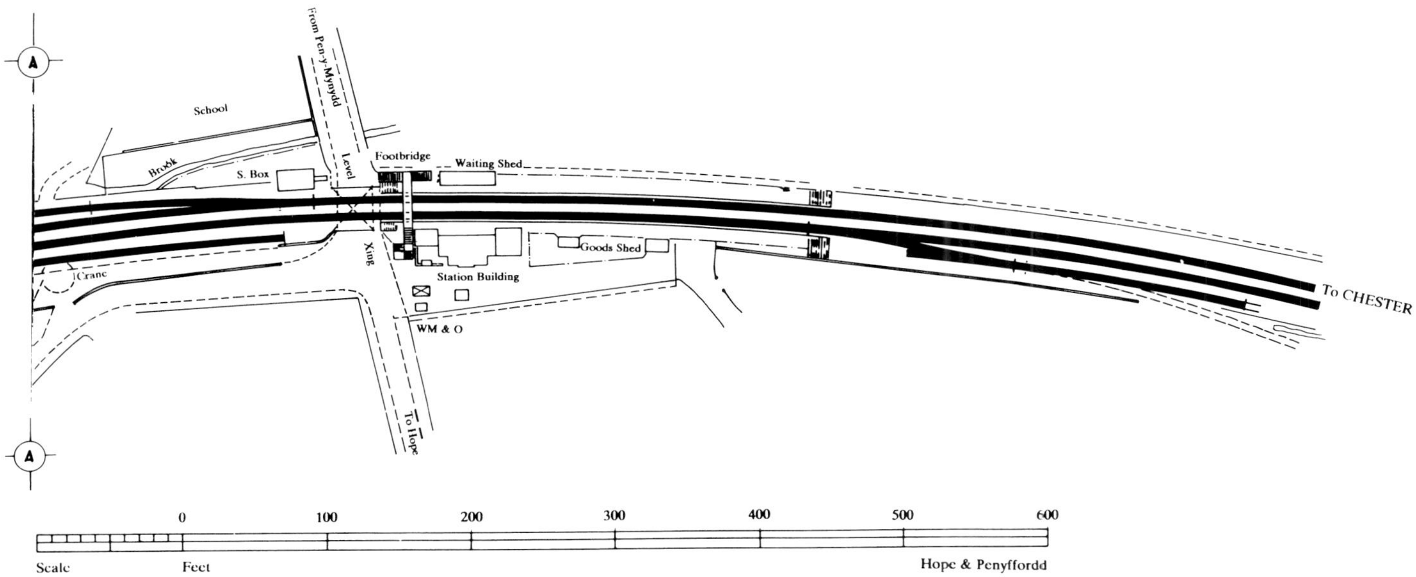

Kinnerton

Two miles 56 chains from Hope & Penyffordd and six miles 23 chains from Chester General, was Kinnerton station, located on the steeply graded Kinnerton bank. The station was of simple construction, consisting of simple platforms with standard "portable" LNWR wooden buildings providing a station office and waiting room on the Down side, and a waiting hut on the Up. At one time there was a trailing siding off the Up line, controlled from a small ground frame, but this was removed before the line lost its passenger services. The 1929 Railway Clearing House Handbook of Stations lists the facilities available to handle goods, passenger and livestock traffic, but what little freight traffic there was seemed restricted by several factors, coal being handled by the local merchant and a very limited amount of livestock. Freight traffic was withdrawn from the station from 5th December 1955. Between Kinnerton and Hope & Penyffordd, on the 1 in 43 rising gradient on the Down side was Kinnerton Sand Siding. The 1910 signal box list shows an all brick signal cabin measuring 11' 0" x 10' 6" on the Down side, which controlled 3 points and 6 signals. However, an undated sketch in the author's possession numbered SW50100 shows a ground frame along side the siding. The siding was included in the September 1961 Freight Working Time Table, but was not listed the following year.

147. Kinnerton. n.d. The Down platform was equally devoid of comfort, although the waiting room was not open to the elements. At one time a small goods yard existed behind the Up platform, protected by signals which were controlled from a six lever frame, but this was removed when the goods yard closed to traffic on 5th December 1955. A track renewal programme was imminent, judging by the concrete sleepers stored on the platform, but few passengers would have been inconvenienced by their presence. Passengers crossed the line by a barrow crossing at the Denbigh end of the platform. *Author's collection.*

146. Kinnerton. 23rd April 1959. The Up platform at Kinnerton, seen from a Chester to Denbigh train. The station was a somewhat basic affair, and comprised two wooden sheds, one serving as a booking office and waiting room, the other as a store. The gradient was severe at this point and in the early days, it was not uncommon for trains to experience great difficulty in restarting on the gradient. On more than one occasion, before block signalling was introduced, and when the time interval system was practiced, stalled trains were run into. *R.J. Buckley.*

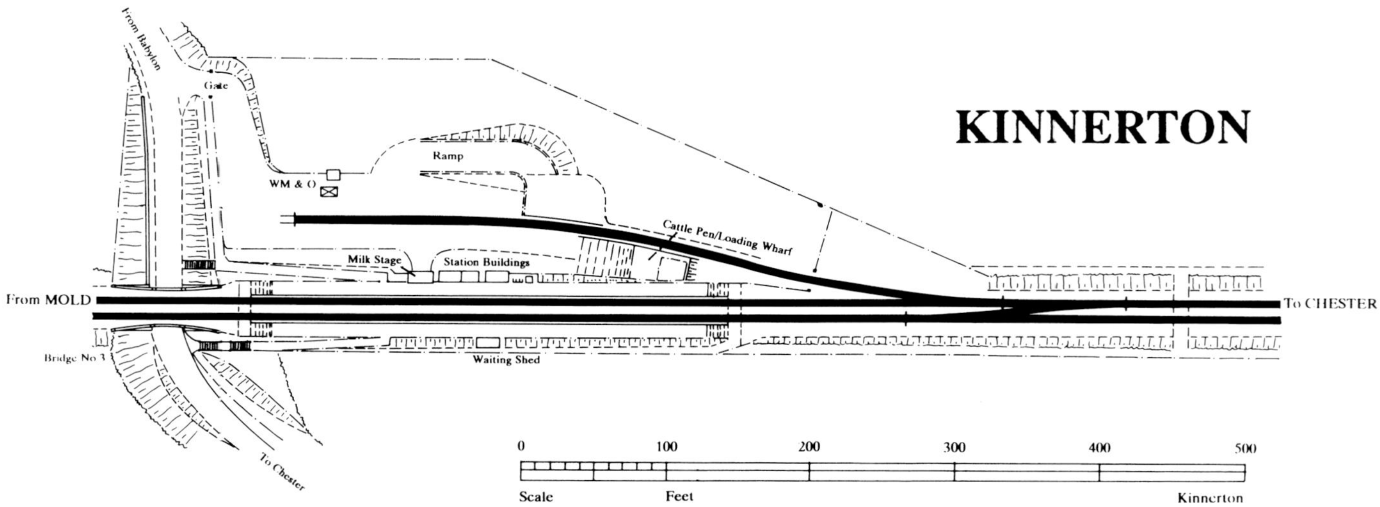

148. Broughton & Bretton. n.d. Taken from the Down platform and looking across the level crossing towards Kinnerton, this view shows the details of the signal box side, together with a view of the Up platform waiting shelter that incorporated an extended roof to give some protection to passengers. The rest of the platform is somewhat devoid of furniture, beyond a single seat , nameboard and lamp posts, minus their lamps. *Author's collection.*

Broughton & Bretton

Originally named 'Broughton' when the line opened, it was changed in April 1861 to Broughton Hall, to avoid confusion with other stations of that name in different parts of the country. It was changed for a third time to Broughton & Bretton on the 1st July 1908. The station closed to all traffic on 4th June 1964.

It was located 1743 yards from Mold Junction No.3 signal box and one and a half miles from Kinnerton at the foot of the first stage of Kinnerton Bank. The main station buildings were located on the Down side, to the same design as most of the other buildings constructed for the Mold Railway. The Up platform had a shelter similar to that at Hope & Penyffordd. Passengers crossed the line from the booking office to the Up platform on the level, alongside the road crossing, where the A549 Chester to Hawarden road crossed the line at the Mold end of the station. The level crossing was controlled from a standard LNWR design all brick cabin at the foot of the Up platform ramp. The box had a set of twenty five levers. A small goods yard was located on the Down side at the Chester end of the platform and sidings were added to the Up side during the second World War, to serve the Vickers aircraft factory. The Premier Artificial Stone Company Ltd. had a siding off the goods yard to their works.

After the line closed to passenger traffic on 30th April 1962, non-advertised workmens passenger trains for the aircraft works continued to work from Chester to Broughton & Bretton at 7.40am, returning in the evenings at 5.10pm (MX), 5.30pm (MO), finally disappearing from the working time table by 15th June 1964. Freight trains continued to work through the station until final closure.

149. Broughton & Bretton. c.1950. The station buildings on the Down platform were of uniform design with others on the former Mold Railway, designed by Francis Thompson, and were similar to the smaller structures built for the Chester & Holyhead Railway. The platforms were of low height, necessitating portable steps being available for passengers. *J.M. Dunn.*

150. Broughton & Bretton. 23rd April 1959. The railway crossed the Chester to Hawarden road on the level at the Mold end of the station, and the gates were operated from the signal cabin that stood on the Up side, and which had a clear view of road traffic in both directions. This was a wooden structure, which housed a 25 lever frame together with the gate operating mechanism. This view was taken from a Chester to Denbigh train. *R.J. Buckley.*

151. Broughton & Bretton. October 1951. Broughton & Bretton station was to the same basic design as many of the stations constructed for the Mold Railway, although there were some minor differences in internal layout. The main building was located on the Down platform. The Up platform had a brick built semi open waiting shelter, although this might have been a replacement structure. During the Second World War, Vickers built an aircraft assembly works behind the Up platform, which brought a huge increase in freight traffic for the works, and which resulted in the building of new private sidings on the Up side at the Chester end of the platform, to serve the works. The domestic goods traffic was located at the same end, but on the Down side. *D. Thompson.*

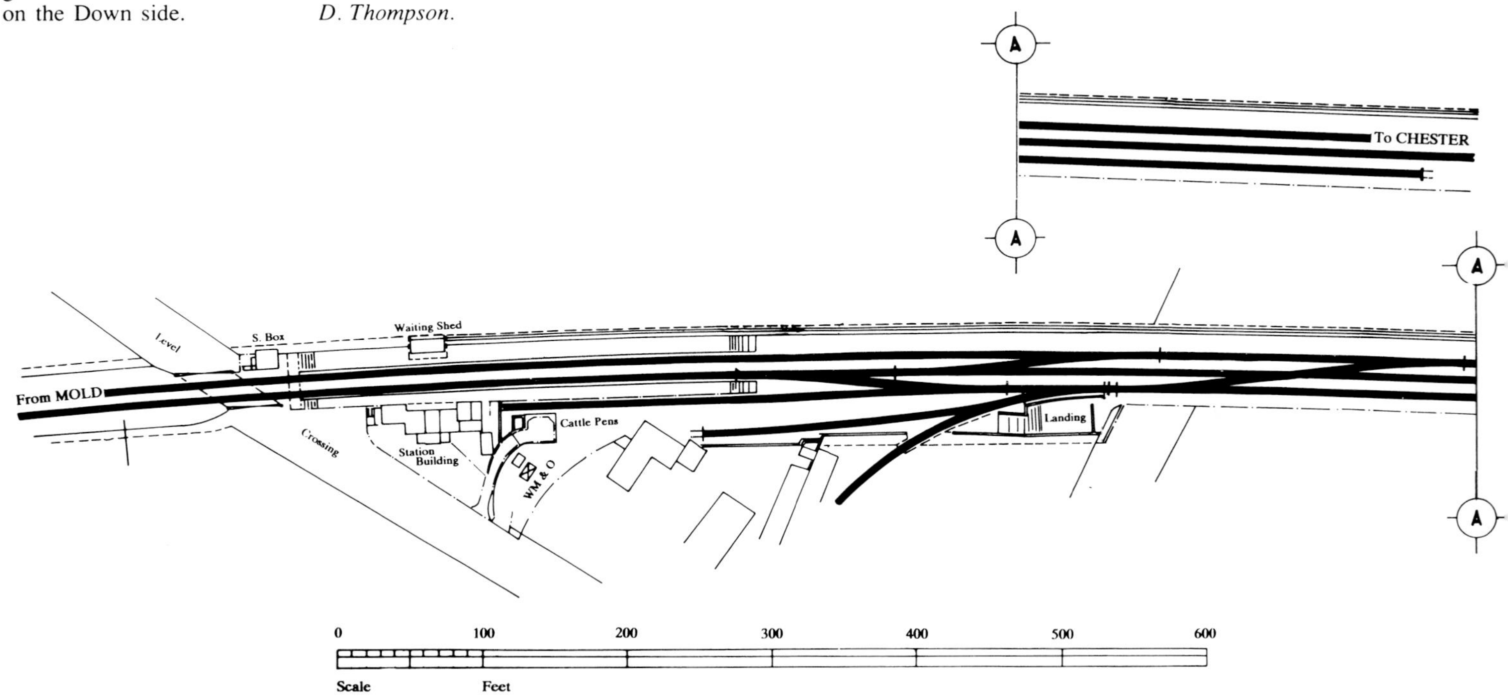

Saltney Ferry.

Probably better known as Mold Junction, which was the location of the sorting sidings for the Chester and North Wales lines of the LNWR, Saltney Ferry was the name of the passenger station which served the small community of Saltney. The station was 3 miles 27 chains from Chester General station and the single island platform was the first station west from Chester, but only served by trains to and from Mold. Coast line trains had no facilities to call there. The platform was about 200ft in length, and access was from Sandycroft Lane that crossed over the line at the eastern end of the complex down a flight of stairs. The Down line passed between the Motive Power depot and the platform, and the Up and Down line to Mold separated the Motive Power yard from the main sorting sidings that ran parallel to the main line. Four signal boxes controlled all traffic. No.1. box was at the Chester end on the Down side. No.2. box was located 483 yards from No.1. box, between the Motive Power yard and the Up & Down lines to Mold. No.3. box was located by the $^{1}/_{2}$ milepost on the Up side of the Mold line, 431 yards from No.2. box and controlled the approach to the station, access to the sidings that ran parallel to the Mold line and the spur to the Down Slow main that formed the third side of the triangle with the coast line. No.2 box was open continuously, whilst No.3. box was opened during the hours that traffic was worked to and from Mold.
There were no facilities for handling local freight at the station, this being dealt with at Chester, Sandycroft or Broughton & Bretton. Passenger traffic ceased on 30th April 1962.

152. Saltney Ferry. 7th October 1966. Another view of the island platform, taken after the station had closed, from Sandycroft Lane, and looking over the motive power yard and the sorting sidings on the Down side of the North Wales main line. The shed had closed on 18th April of the same year, and the depot tracks were used to store loco coal. The shed survives to this day, but its rail connection has been severed, and the building and yard are now scrap metal premises. *D. Thompson.*

153. Saltney Ferry. 1952. The platform at Saltney Ferry was a very basic affair, consisting of a rather short length island platform on the Chester & Holyhead Up and Down Slow Lines, with passenger access off Sandycroft Lane, by means of a flight of stairs. At one time there was a shelter at the foot of the stairs, but this was removed some time before the station closed. The platform adjoined Mold Junction loco shed (6B). *L&GRP No.26487.*

154. Chester General Station. 1957. Most trains for Denbigh, Ruthin or Corwen departed from bay platform No.1., often referred to as 'The Denbigh Bay'. which was in the older part of the station. Here, the stock of a Denbigh train is being propelled into the bay. In the formation is a corridor full brake van which was used to store the evening mail from Denbigh on the return journey. Through the arches are Bay Platforms 2 which, adjoins platform 1, and Bay platform 3, which was used mostly by the GWR/Western Region. Across from No.3 Bay is No.4 Platform, which was the main through platform for departures along the North Wales Coast. A wide footbridge extended across the tracks to all platforms, and also to the exit on Hoole Road. This was removed during station reconstruction in the late 1960's. Eventually No.1 and 2 platforms were removed. *G.H.Platt.*

155. Chester General station. 1962. The exterior of the station was an imposing structure, shown to good advantage in this view. Note the cars, used mainly for taxis, in the station forcourt. *G.H.Platt.*

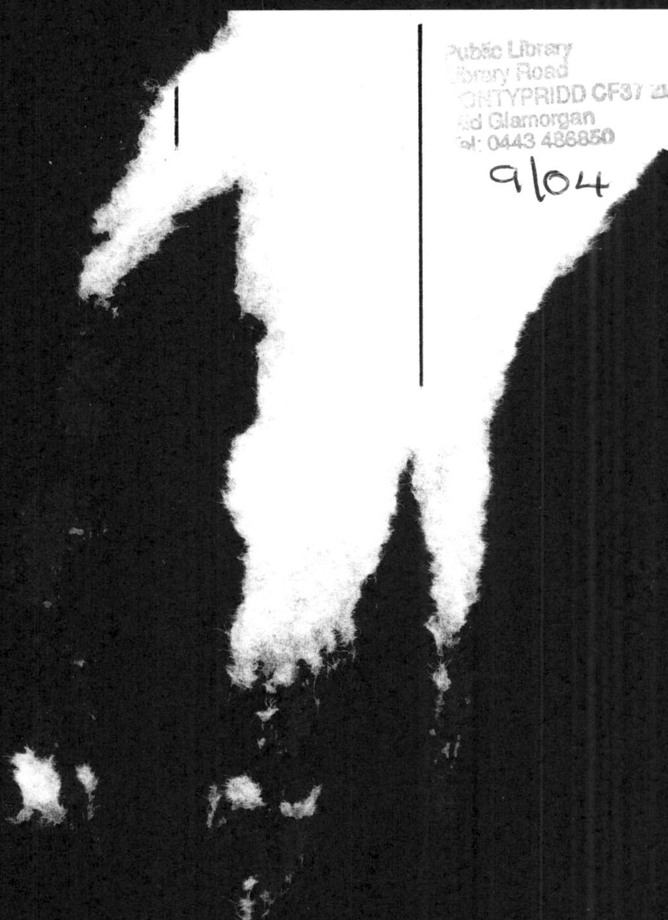